FLYING THE TYRANT

THE DECLASSIFIED STORY OF FLYING SADDAM HUSSEIN,
KEEPING SECRETS, AND ESCAPING ASSASSINATION

LAUREN UNGELDI

MOHAMMED SULAIMAN

Flying the Tyrant:
The Declassified Story of Flying Saddam Hussein, Keeping Secrets, and Escaping Assassination
by Lauren Ungeldi and Mohammed Sulaiman

Ebook ISBN: 979-8-9876717-0-2
Paperback ISBN: 979-8-9876717-1-9
Hardcover ISBN: 979-8-9876717-2-6

Copyright © 2023 by Lauren Ungeldi. All rights reserved.

Formatted by Ben Wolf
www.benwolf.com/editing-services/

Cover design by Jenneth Dyck
jennethd1@gmail.com

All rights reserved. Non-commercial interests may reproduce portions of this book without the express written permission of the author, provided the text does not exceed 500 words. For longer quotations or commercial concerns, please contact the author.

Commercial interests: No part of this publication may be reproduced in any form, stored in a retrieval system, or transmitted in any form by any means—electronic, photocopy, recording, or otherwise—without prior written permission of the author, except as provided by the United States of America copyright law.

Printed in the United States of America.

PRAISE FOR FLYING THE TYRANT_

"Spectacular, fast-paced, a wild ride!"

- **Geraint Jones**, *New York Times* and *Sunday Times* bestselling author

---

"You are holding classified information that was pivotal in an Iranian assassination case that I was directly involved in."

- **Hamody Jasim**, author of *Terrorist Whisperer*, former U.S. Spy

---

"Flying the Tyrant is a powerful and fascinating look into the tyrannical life of Saddam Hussein, masterfully told through the window of his closest circle. This gripping tale is a shocking look into what the brutal dictator's life behind closed doors was really like, and Illuminates the hold he had on the country we spent over a decade in fighting."

- **Mike Ritland**, former Navy SEAL, *New York Times* bestseller, entrepreneur

CONTENTS_

Author's Note	1
Chapter 1	7
Chapter 2	23
Chapter 3	41
Chapter 4	63
Chapter 5	85
Chapter 6	101
Chapter 7	117
Chapter 8	131
Chapter 9	149
Chapter 10	161
Chapter 11	171
Chapter 12	179
Chapter 13	195
Acknowledgments	199
Also by Lauren Ungeldi	201
About the Authors	205

AUTHOR'S NOTE_

As an author and ghostwriter, I've had the distinct pleasure of meeting a wide variety of individuals from around the world. I've worked with war heroes, politicians, entrepreneurs, survivors, creators, and leaders who have lived extraordinary lives that deserve to be highlighted on the page.

But I can tell you beyond a shadow of a doubt that Mr. Sulaiman is one of the most incredible people I have ever had the pleasure of meeting and working with. Our connection was unlikely from the beginning —a dozen improbable events culminating at just the right time to bring us together.

My first book, *Legion Rising*, was for Jeff Morris—a company commander in the Iraq War. After the book launched, Jeff was interviewed by former Navy SEAL, entrepreneur, and podcast host Mike Ritland. On air, he told the story of a particular firefight that took place in Baghdad during his deployment where he strategically fought to save a handful of young, local Iraqis.

As it so happens, on a previous episode of the show, Mike had conducted an interview with a man by the name of Hamody Jasim a.k.a The Terrorist Whisperer. Hamody was recruited by US Intelligence after saving an American military officer who was nearly abducted by al-Qaeda as a young Iraqi boy and went on to become a best-selling author and film director later in life.

And because life is the greatest author of all time, weaving together real storylines and plots better than any fiction writer ever could, Hamody Jasim just happened to be one of the young Iraqis that Jeff Morris fought to save and protect that day. They had been there together on Haifa Street that day.

In the midst of fear, sweat, blood, and dust, the two men didn't speak. They didn't commit to memory any distinguishing features of the other's face. They simply survived that day. Neither man expected to meet the other again. But fate had a plot twist. Both men became authors. Both men were interviewed on the same talk show. Both men realized who the other was.

After reuniting and exchanging books, Jeff introduced me, his writer, to Hamody. We connected instantly.

"I think I have your next book project," Hamody messaged me out of the blue one day. *"He's the former pilot for Saddam Hussein. Here's his phone number."*

When I dialed that number and waited for the phone to ring, I wasn't sure what to expect. I was about to speak to a man who had spent years of his life close to one of the most infamous dictators in history.

The voice that greeted me on the other side was kind, gentle, and filled with the gentlemanly charm of an era gone by. Our connection was effortless, and within a month, the work began.

We opened the vault of Sulaiman's memories and began to pull them out together, one by one. Flying into a sandstorm under death threat. Witnessing a top-secret meeting between the Israeli Prime Minister and Saddam Hussein that almost cost Sulaiman his life. Seeing the dictator in his underwear. Fleeing Iraq after narrowly escaping an assassination attempt. Landing in Mogadishu, Somalia, in the middle of a military coup d'état. Starting completely over as an immigrant to the US and rebuilding his life from the ground up after being forced to give up his career.

It was an intricate plot with enough twists and turns to make any action novelist proud. But it was all true. The man I was speaking with had lived it all. But somehow these extraordinary and even horrifying things that he had been through had not left him calloused, unfeeling, or cynical toward life. Instead, he carried an impenetrable sense of positivity. It seemed that his near-death experiences had unlocked the secrets of living life well. He worked hard both in business and as a consultant for the US military, but he rose every day before dawn to jog several miles and watch the sun rise, play classical piano, eat with friends, hug his children and grandchildren, and savor the simple pleasures of life.

The time I spent with him inspired me. His easygoing

attitude rubbed off on me. It put my own life into perspective. Reminded me of what matters in life, made the big things seem small. For that, I'll always be grateful. It was a joy to immerse myself in his world, to "become" him, to live inside his mind, to listen to his thoughts, and to capture his stories and bring them to life on the page.

This book is not a book about politics or the merits of war. It is a book about a man who lived an uncommon life and lived to tell about it. These pages reveal first-person accounts of classified meetings and events that took place during Saddam's reign that have never before been shared. It explores the complexities of what it is like to be a good man and an accomplished pilot who is forced to serve a brutal dictator. It's a celebration of the courage it takes to leave everything behind, start over, and create a new life as an immigrant in another country.

There have been many books that highlight the stories of American men and women who served in the military throughout the years of conflict in the Middle East, but few stories have been told of noble Iraqis, like Sulaiman, who were forced to navigate the challenges that come with serving a heartless tyrant under a repressive regime. Sulaiman's story gives a powerful, eye-opening, and deeply personal look into these experiences and provides a unique perspective to an extraordinary time in history.

I designed this book to be a fast read, an immersive experience. There are certain names, places, and dates that have been changed or left vague on purpose since there are still people alive today who could be affected by careless disclosure of these details.

The details in this book are portraits created by the brushstrokes of recollection and memories that have endured throughout the years. We strove for accuracy and did our best to recount the story with precision. Even so, there will always be the possibility that we got it wrong somewhere due to the limitations of the mind trying to remember the past. However, as the reader, you can count on the fact that I worked hard to create a book filled with authenticity that captures Sulaiman's remarkable story and allows you to connect with the wonderful man that I have had the pleasure of working with these past few years.

Now more than ever, our nation is hungry to understand the past from a broader perspective and illuminate the stories of individuals who experience the world from a different point of view.

Sulaiman's story makes us reconsider what we thought we knew about this significant time in history, challenges our preconceived notions, and causes us to turn inward and ask ourselves tough questions.

What if you knew you could create a better future for your family if you had to take a simple job for a cruel and powerful tyrant?

What would you do if you opened your front door and found a death threat under your feet or witnessed a top-secret mission that could cost you your life?

These are the questions we will explore together.

So, with that, it's time to get down to it.
Read on.

CHAPTER ONE_

I remember my body humming with the vibration of the plane beneath me. My hands grasping the wheel, a connection like electricity through my body. The power, the freedom of flying in open air rushed through me and it made my heart race.

I climbed higher and higher, above the clouds.

I am above the clouds.

I could almost feel the cold, rushing air on my face.

A thunderous sound erupted suddenly, followed by sirens blaring. Something was wrong. I'd heard about flights like this. Where things go very, very wrong. It was happening to me.

It's happening to me.

"Engine fire, engine fire!" I yelled.

My heart began to thud like a hammer. I could see black smoke billowing, and my body shifted as the aircraft began to spin out of control. I thought of the hard ground below.

It was time to make a choice. I could jump or I could die.

I didn't look, I didn't think, I just jumped.

For a moment, I felt weightless as I floated through open space and sky. I caught a glimpse of my parachute above me.

It will hold me. It will save me. I'll float gently to the ground.

The next thing I felt was the surface of the earth against my flesh and bones, merciless and unbending as I thudded to the ground. My body flopped like a rag doll, and pain shot through every part of my body.

I shrieked.

Pain.

Pain.

Pain everywhere.

Then arms were around me. I was being lifted. My head pounded and my lips felt numb. Hot tears poured out of my eyes and down my face, salt in wounds.

I was in a car.

I was in a hospital.

Voices around me, talking about me.

"He jumped from a rooftop and took a hard fall on the ground below." I heard the voice of my father.

"He jumped?" The doctor looked in my direction with a concerned look.

"You have to understand that I am a pilot. My son loves to pretend that he can fly," said my father, worried. "He was holding on to an umbrella when he jumped. I believe he thought it was a parachute that would hold him."

I closed my eyes as if the darkness would make the pain go

away. I could still hear my father's voice:

"Doctor, he's only six years old."

And then it clicked. Like pieces of a puzzle suddenly snapping into place. I remembered what I had done. The umbrella in the corner of my parents' room. Me grabbing it and pressing down on the metal button. Jumping when it swelled and popped open over my head, reminding me of the pictures I had seen of parachutes.

Snatches and bits of my father's stories playing through my mind. Pieces I had gathered from the conversations that surrounded me and fueled my imagination. My legs climbed up to the rooftop; my mind told me I was flying. Higher and higher. Then suddenly danger came for me like I always knew it would. Like all the stories I had heard so many times before.

And then came the jump.

I received stitches that day and the doctors watched me closely for swelling in the brain. I made it out bruised but in one piece, having learned a lesson I would never forget: *umbrellas are not parachutes.*

The first sound I can remember is the hum of a plane engine. The first feeling was the vibration of the cockpit. The first sight was the legs of my father on either side of me as I sat in his lap, reaching for the controls.

He let me grab on with both hands. His hands, then mine. Gripping the wheel, feeling the power it held.

Some people talk about being destined to do something in life; they talk of having a purpose or calling. I'm not a religious man so I cannot speak to the will of God for my life, but I can tell you this: I was born to fly.

Just as surely as I know that my name is Mohammed Sulaiman. That I was born in Iraq. That I love my mother and respect my father. I know that I was born to fly.

It is in my blood and in my veins. Woven into the fabric of my being.

I am, I always was, and I always will be a pilot.

I was born on Royal Air Force Station Habbaniya, more commonly known as RAF. About fifty-five miles west of Baghdad in modern-day Iraq, on the banks of the Euphrates near Lake Habbaniya. I was flying in my father's lap before I could read or write. My childhood was filled with memories of cockpits and airstrips, the sound of planes taking off and landing.

My father was Lieutenant-General Adel Suleiman Dawood Al-Rawi, a powerful and legendary pilot in the Iraqi Army. He trained at Feltwell, an Elementary Flying Base, then transferred to a diversion course on Chevron Hawker Air Force Base. In 1963, he was sent to Britain for an advanced course in aviation and attended the Minor Staff Course for Squadron Commanders in the United States of America for six months.

In 1963, my father participated in the February 8 Revolution, also known as the Ramadan Revolution, a military coup d'état in Iraq, by the Ba'ath Party's Iraq-wing, which overthrew the Prime Minister of Iraq, Abd al-Karim Qasim, that lasted for two days. My father was in command of the 6th Squadron and carried out three sorties against the Ministry of Defense.

In 1966, my father was imprisoned with several other pilots following this failed coup. That same year, the Iraqi Prime

Minister gave him the assignment of bombing a radio station that broadcasts from the Republican Palace, and he refused the order because of the repercussions this action would undoubtedly cause and the danger of these bombs. He was given the position of Secretary of the Air Force in the Office of the Ministry of Defense.

My father was a legend. Larger than life. He commanded respect in every room he entered, and our home was no exception.

My father was not religious like my mother. He didn't fast during Ramadan. He drank. He listened to all kinds of music. Our family believed in God. Believed that all people are human and should be treated equally. My father taught me to respect the practices of our more religious friends and family. If it was fasting time, I did not flaunt my plate of food. If it was time for prayer, I honored the ones who prayed.

I asked my father once why he was not religious.

"Son, I do not need the fear of hell or the promise of heaven to motivate me to be a good person here and now."

This was only one of the many reasons that my father was my hero. They called my father the King Hunter. His stories of flying and his near brushes with death reached my ears when I was barely old enough to understand, and they filled me with a sense of anticipation. I would be that pilot someday. And so, my childhood became a waiting game, waiting for the day that my body would catch up and become who I already was on the inside: a pilot.

Until the day I became a pilot like my father, my imagination made aircrafts out of anything and everything. I took the bits of dough my mother gave me to play with while she cooked and made a body and wings from it. I removed shoes from my feet and reached them high into the sky, believing that they were the mighty planes that my father flew. I spent hours at the top of the tree in my family's backyard, a pillow from my bed beneath me, pretending to fly. I put cooking pots on my head to serve as my helmet until I worked up the gumption to steal my dad's crash helmet from his bedroom and wear it when he was not around.

These memories marked my early childhood, living on Habbaniya Airbase. I had two brothers, Farid and Samer. Farid was older and Samer was younger but not by much. We were close and played endlessly together, along with the other families that lived on the airbase. We spent the hot Iraqi summers shooting birds with BB guns or swimming in the pool, laughing and trying to form human aircrafts with our arms and legs. My brothers knew that they would be pilots just as I did. And the other boys knew that they would be exactly who their fathers were. We thought of nothing but following in our fathers' footsteps.

In middle school, my father moved our family to Baghdad. He secured a loan and purchased a home in a new subdivision on the edge of town. Other families from the airbase were doing the same thing, which meant that my friends and classmates stayed the same. Not far from our house, a mosque was being built. Every day, I looked up at the Minaret, the tower from which the call to prayer sounded five times each day by a muezzin, or *crier*. These towers are always connected with a mosque and typically have one or more balconies open.

It would be a perfect place to send one of my homemade airplanes on a flight.

Making airplanes had become something of an art form for me. It started with scraps of paper, tiny, folded slips sent across rooms and over furniture. As time passed, they got bigger and bigger. Every discarded cardboard box or piece of Styrofoam was like a treasure to me. I spent hours constructing the body and wings. Every model I had made before served as a syllabus of lessons learned and understanding gained to make the next one better.

When my father would take me to the airbase with him, I would steal a copy of the airplane magazines provided for the pilots there and stuff them beneath my shirt. I'd try not to look guilty as I walked around with the cool, sleek pages pressed against the skin of my belly. The moment I stepped off the airbase I knew the magazines would be mine to study, and it was the best feeling in the world. I used them as guides to construct airplanes. I couldn't read the English words, but I could study the pictures. And study I did. I pored over those pages, planning and strategizing on how I could make my cardboard and Styrofoam into an aircraft worthy of flight.

One day I was certain that I had it. I had spent hours studying the magazines, fine tuning every aspect of its construction. It had a wingspan of more than six feet, and I was proud of it. I waited patiently for a windy day when I would take her on her first flight. Finally, the perfect day came. One of my friends helped me carry it to the top of the Minaret. Sweat beaded down our temples from the thick July heat. Finally, I was in position.

I let it go.

And it took off. The wings caught the wind in just the way I hoped it would. It glided and soared. For fifteen minutes it flew, longer than any aircraft I had ever made, and it made its landing at the doorstep of a neighbor's house. I took off running to retrieve it. When I arrived, panting and red faced at my neighbor's door, my neighbor was already outside, looking it over.

"Did you make this?" the neighbor lady asked in disbelief.

"I did," I said with my sweaty head held high.

The neighbor lady looked shocked. "Show it to me, my boy. I want to see."

I held it out for her to examine, eager for someone to inspect my work.

"This is very good, my son, very good."

I swelled with pride at the sound of my neighbor's praise. She offered us water and sent us on our way, and I ran away feeling proud. I would make an even better one.

I toiled even longer on my next model. Every element had to be just perfect. My shoulders bent and my eyes strained as I worked tirelessly on it. And then the day came when it was ready for its first flight.

I threw it into the wind, and the wings caught the moving air beautifully. Up, up, up it went. I was so enthralled with it that I barely noticed the sound of a plane engine getting closer and closer. And then I saw it.

My dad, inside his aircraft, had dipped down and was flying near my homemade plane.

"No, no, no!" I screamed.

But there was no one to hear and nothing to do.

My father's plane plowed right through my cardboard one, shredding it into a million pieces.

It would have made for a good story had I not been so heartbroken. All I could see was the hours of hard work and toil lying on the sandy ground. And I cried that day.

By the time I was a young teenager, I graduated from the seat between my dad's legs and was allowed to fly with the assistance of my father. My father handed me the controls and allowed me to pilot the takeoff and landing by myself. By the time I was fifteen, I was successfully flying all on my own. My dad kept a watchful eye over me as I started the engines and took off. He took care of communications but allowed me complete control of the aircraft. Once in the air, my father would instruct me on how to do maneuvers, teaching me skills and techniques. And then I'd land.

I was flying before I could drive.

During my years as a teenager, there was talk around dinner tables and behind closed doors about our nation's newest president, Saddam Hussein. Saddam took over when former president al-Bakr attempted to unite Iraq and Syria—a move that would have left Saddam effectively powerless. Saddam had already been the *de facto* head of Iraq for several years, but he forced al-Bakr to resign and became president of Iraq on July 16, 1979. Less than a week later, he called an assembly of the Ba'ath Party, which espoused Ba'athism, a mix of Arab nationalism and Arab socialism.

Almost immediately Saddam entered a war with Iran. Open warfare officially began on September 22, 1980, when Iraqi armed forces invaded western Iran along the countries' joint border, though many Iraqis believed that the war had begun earlier that month when Iran shelled several border posts.

The roots of the war can be found in a number of political disputes between Iraq and Iran as well as territorial disputes. Iraq wanted to take control of the rich oil-producing Iranian border region of Khūzestān. Saddam also wanted to reassert his country's sovereignty over both banks of the Shaṭṭ al-ʿArab, a river formed by the Tigris and Euphrates rivers, which historically served as the border between the two countries.

My father was not a deeply political man, but he hated Saddam. He was a pilot, first and foremost. And he loved his job. Flying was in his blood, the same blood that he gave to me. He was gifted and skilled at it. It was all he'd ever wanted to do. He followed orders just as all good military men do, but politics weren't the primary motivating factor in his choice to be a pilot. But with Saddam's rise to power, I heard the frustrations of my father and other military men voiced often in conversation. They felt that Saddam was stupid, corrupt, and evil. The idea that he had risen to power was a deep source of anger. Everything they said was true, but it scared me to hear them say it.

We had heard the stories of the brutal repercussions that were dealt to those who dared to speak out against Saddam. It seemed that he had eyes and ears everywhere. But my father couldn't hold in his hatred for this brutal dictator who had so unfairly come to power in our nation. I understood my father's anger, but the sound of those sentiments forming into audible words struck fear into my heart.

"Dad, please," I begged him. "Please don't talk this way. If word gets out that you are speaking in this way, he will kill you. He will kill us all."

But my father couldn't suppress it.

I lived in constant fear that someone would hear him, that somehow his strong feelings and oppositions would fall on the wrong ears.

The moment I graduated high school I headed straight to the Air Force hospital to get my full physical examination so I could join the Air Force. I passed. On November 1, 1982, I officially joined the Iraqi Air Force. Within a few months I was flying solo after just two or three rides with an instructor—a privilege that typically takes at least ten to fifteen successful flights to earn, and I felt proud. I felt as though I had been waiting all my life to truly live.

And now I could live.

But it seemed that every day we heard reports of the inhumane and barbaric acts that were taking place at the bidding of our new president. Rage over the decisions Saddam made and things that he did boiled up inside me, and I found myself unable to hold it inside. The anger came spilling out in words that sounded like my father. I voiced these feelings quietly, secretly, only to the ears of trusted friends. But in the hours that followed, a knot would form in my stomach, and my mind would race.

What if someone heard me? What if someone said something? What if my thoughtless words were the reason for the death of my father, my mother, my brothers? Myself?

I vowed to hold my feeling in, to never speak of them again.

But my hatred for Saddam's brutality and the incredulity I felt at Saddam's stupidity and greed rose within me like a shaken can of soda, waiting to explode.

Not long after, we received word that my mom's first cousin, who had served in the Iraqi Army Aviation, was forced to flee Iraq after word got out that he had voiced opposition against Saddam. My family had a deep friendship with my mom's first cousin's family. His sons were the same ages as me and my brothers. The middle son of my mom's first cousin was my closest and best childhood friend. We would spend hours in the pool, splashing and laughing. We also would go hiking and biking together.

And now their father was on the run. He fled through the north of Iraq, Saddam's men in close pursuit behind him, and he made it across the border. He kept moving until he made it to Germany where he settled.

Unable to catch my mom's first cousin, Saddam sent word through his brother, also my mom's first cousin, that if he did not return, he would begin killing his sons, one by one. He did not return.

And Saddam did just as he had promised. He killed all three of my mom's first cousin's sons, one of which was my best childhood friend. This incident struck fear into all of us. The reality that we were living under a brutal dictatorship sunk in with a suffocating sense of fear. Every move I made, every word I uttered I did so with a sense of paranoia. Always looking over my shoulder, always alert, always cautious.

I continued my flying courses in Jordan after flight school, devoting myself to honing my abilities and developing my skills as a pilot. I wanted to be the best.

My quest for perfection was accompanied by a desire to test my limits and see what I was capable of. I loved the rush that came with attempting a tricky maneuver or performing a trick in the air for everyone on the ground to see.

Flying made me feel powerful. It made me feel daring. It made me feel alive.

On one day, I spotted a young couple from the air, parked between the bushes, leaning against a car, kissing. They thought they would be undisturbed in their hidden rendezvous spot.

I smirked. It was an opportunity for fun that I couldn't pass up, and I flew down low, right over the couple.

They looked in my direction but didn't react much.

And then I did it again.

And again.

And again.

I could see the rage boiling on the guy's face, even from the air. He shook his fists at me and yelled.

I passed over the couple yet again.

The guy charged to the trunk of his vehicle and produced an AK47 machine gun and pointed it at me. I flew low and then went up again and stayed in the area until the couple got back in their vehicle and returned to the highway.

"Gotcha," I said with a wicked grin.

There wasn't anything the guy could do to me now that he was driving on the main road.

And I bothered him all the way back to Baghdad.

On January 6, 1984, I graduated as a lieutenant. My parents were immensely proud to see me take my place in the family legacy of incredible pilots, alongside my father and older brother.

But even as I celebrated this personal victory, there was no escaping the reality that tensions between Iran and Iraq were only continuing to escalate. Iran backed an Al-Dawah party insurgency against Saddam Hussein's Ba'athist government in Iraq. Al-Dawah had relocated its headquarters to Tehran, the capital of Iran, and bombed the Iraqi Embassy in Beirut in December 1981, the first of its international attacks. It was also believed that the Al-Dawah party was behind the bombing of the US embassy in Kuwait as well as other installations as punishment of Kuwait's, America's, and France's military and financial assistance to Iraq in its war against Iran.

Members of the Al-Dawah party placed bombs inside Iraqi air bases and timed them to detonate. Three aircrafts were lost as a result. Not long after, two bombs were placed inside the Air Force college but were detected and defused in time before they exploded.

They also placed another bomb inside of an aircraft in Saddam Airbase.

And on June 23, 1984, my older brother, Faried, piloted that plane.

The bomb went off while my brother was up in the air, exploding the entire cockpit in front of him. He lived for three hours after the crash, just long enough to tell the story of what happened.

And then he died.

News of my brother's death hit my family with crushing force. He was young and driven. Full of hopes and dreams for his future. Smiling and laughing with us one day. Gone the next.

My father tried to remain strong, but on more than one occasion, I found my father in his room bent over a picture of my brother, tears streaming down his face. My mother did not cope well at all. Upon hearing the news, she wept, and I'm not sure she ever stopped. In the weeks and months that followed, she cried almost continuously. Hour after hour, day after day. The smiling mother who used to prepare dolma and biryani with a light in her eye, who grinned wide as she brought out three-foot-thick trays piled high with kibbeh to feed us seemed all but gone.

After several months, my father took my mother to the hospital, worried about her mental health as she slipped deeper and deeper into depression. They administered electroconvulsive therapy, electrically inducing a seizure in an attempt to manage her mental disorder.

But nothing could bring her son back.

My entire career as a pilot was still ahead of me. And perhaps my brother's death should have made me question my path or feel afraid to fly.

But it didn't.

I knew my brother loved flying as much as I did. It had been in my brother's blood just as much as it was in mine.

"You're lucky to have died in a plane, my brother," I whispered. "You died doing what you love. I can only hope that when my time comes, I, too, will die in the sky."

CHAPTER TWO_

Fresh out of college, it was time for me to find my place in the workforce. As a career pilot, the ladder toward success and high-powered positions extended above me, every rung empty and waiting for me to climb. My entire life revolved around flying. I lived it, I ate it, I breathed it. I invested everything I had into school. I studied hard, ensuring that I passed every exam with flying colors. I was prepared and ready. Ready to put my head down, ready to earn my way to the top.

But the climb happened much faster than I expected.

My father's position as Secretary of the Air Force in the Office of the Ministry of Defense, made him responsible for overseeing all things related to aviation and the entire Iraqi Air Force. And my dad was determined to give me a shot at flying for the VIP squadron.

The VIP squadron oversaw transporting members of the

royal family, top-ranking military officials, prime ministers, foreign dignitaries, dictators, presidents, and the very man himself, Saddam Hussein. Being a pilot on the VIP squad was the dream position that every young graduate like me hoped to have. There was great honor in getting to fly powerful and noteworthy people such as these.

It also provided incredible travel opportunities. Not only did the pilot fly the president or general or dignitary or member of the royal family wherever they needed to go, but while they conducted their business, the pilot was given a generous per diem and was allowed to rest, shop, and sightsee while he waited for the flight back. VIP pilots were paid handsomely, fed well, and showered with gifts. But it was a difficult position and hard to secure. Only the most skilled, experienced, and highly vetted pilots were allowed to fly. It wasn't a place for fresh-faced graduates like me who possessed relatively little experience.

But my dad was determined. He believed in my talent and didn't want me to spend years in some unknown flight squad. So he put me up for consideration to be a part of the VIP squad. The thought of flying such powerful individuals made me nervous but excited. I knew I was a good pilot. I had been flying since I was barely a teenager. But flying on the VIP squad was no small matter.

Soon after being put up for consideration, I was forced headlong into a severe and rigorous background check. If I sneezed wrong or masturbated in my closet as a teenager, I promise you they would have known. The questionnaire form was sixty pages long. It was no small task to come up with sixty pages of questions for one human being to answer. They asked about every single part of my life. And when I say every single part, I mean *every single part*. Not only did they want to know every detail about my family, extended family, and circle of friends, they wanted to know every personal and intimate detail of my entire life.

They asked if I liked having sex. They asked *how* I liked having sex. They asked about my religious beliefs. They asked about my uncles. And then my uncles' wives. And then my uncles' wives' families. I had to track down family members I had never met, whose names I didn't even know. By the time I finished the last page and sent it to the palace for review, I was exhausted and nervous. It seemed unlikely that I would get the position. If I did, I knew I could look forward to filling that probing questionnaire every single year.

If I had been any regular graduate right out of school, I wouldn't have stood a chance of getting onto the squad. But my father worked right under the Minister of Defense. When my dad pulled strings, it was as if the Minister had. When my dad said something, it was as if the Minister had said it. This meant I had a sliver of a chance of flying on the VIP squad.

It wasn't long before I got word that my application had been accepted and approved. I could hardly believe it. The only hurdle left to overcome was the medical examination, which was known for being just as rigorous as the questionnaire had been.

I remember sitting nervously in the Air Force hospital, waiting for my name to be called. I had a real shot at getting on the VIP squad, and I didn't want anything to ruin that chance.

Please don't find anything. Please don't find anything wrong with me.

I sat up straight as if good posture would somehow improve my chances of passing the medical examination with flying colors. I wasn't prepared for what followed. I'm not sure that a human body has ever been so closely inspected as I was that day. They looked at every hair on my head; they probed with lights deep into my ears. They looked between every toe for signs of fungus or even an infected toenail. They spread my fingers and did the same. They listened to my lungs and heart. They looked up into my nostrils as if they thought they would find gold there.

Many people failed that examination. If you had so much as a little fungus or warts between your toes, you were out. It didn't matter how good of a pilot you were. It didn't matter that your bare feet would never touch the inside of the plane. If you were flying for the VIP squad, you had to be the picture of perfect health. Not a spot in your eye or a rash on your backside or an allergy.

Clear. Clear. Clear.

The results of every test I took came back clear.

I was one of only a handful of others that managed to pass the exam.

I was also fortunate that though my family was not deeply religious, I had been born Sunni and not Shia. Shia and Sunni are the two major denominations of Islam. Following the death of the Islamic prophet Muhammad in AD 632, people began to choose sides, and a divide was created. A dispute over succession and a debate emerged about who should be his successor and spread across various parts of the world.

Both sides agreed that Allah is the one true God and that Muhammad was his messenger, but one group felt that Muhammad's successor should be someone in his bloodline, while the other felt a pious individual who would follow the Prophet's customs was acceptable. The first group eventually became the Shiites and the second became the Sunnis. Of course, this is an extremely over-simplified description. There are many complex dynamics that create the divide between the two belief systems.

The point is that Saddam did not trust anyone from Shia descent. He ensured that they played no direct role in the government. What's more, his regime sought to control and suppress its Shia population. Many clerics who were said to be of Iranian origin were expelled to Iran. Iraqi school curriculum taught only Sunni Islam and were forbidden to teach Shia.

As Saddam waged war against Iran, he also targeted Iraq's Shia population by accusing them of having connections with Iran and not being patriotic.

It seemed crazy to me that such small religious differences were of such great importance in our government. I had been raised to respect the religious practices of others, to see all humans as children of God and equal. But this was not the way of Saddam. And I found myself grateful that I had been born Sunni.

And then came the day when I received the news.

I was in.

I had been accepted on the VIP squad, and at twenty-two

years old, I would soon be flying some of the most powerful leaders and dictators in the entire world. I couldn't believe it.

The first position I was given was as copilot, or P2. I remember sitting in the copilot's chair on one of my first fights, waiting to see who we would be piloting. It was all so new and surreal.

Onto the field walked General Abdul Jabbar Khalil Shanshal, one of Iraq's oldest senior officers, who also served as the war minister for a very long period, Minister of Military Affairs, and Chief of Staff. He was a legend, a relic, an icon in the Iraqi military. But on that day, he boarded the plane looking terrified. His back was bent, and his face was squeezed tightly. His face was white as a sheet. We would be flying him all the way to Moscow.

I looked at my squadron leader, Major Awof, and he gave me a knowing look. General Jabbar had an intense fear of flying. *Phobia* may be a better suited term for it. I watched as General Jabbar stepped inside the plane and made his way to his seat. He was visibly shaking, as if death was peering over his shoulder. I don't know if the fear was the result of age, PTSD, or if it was something he had always battled. But Major Awof didn't have to speak a word for us both to know that this flight better go without a hitch. We settled in and began going through the preflight procedures.

Suddenly a cry from the cabin sounded through the entire plane.

"Allah! Allah!" General Jabbar cried "My God, my God."

The door between the cabin and the cockpit was open, and I snapped my head back to see what had caused such an outcry.

I locked eyes with General Jabbar. The shouts subsided, and General Jabbar held my gaze for a moment, looking as if he wanted to say something but couldn't find the words. Tormented eyes shone out from General Jabbar's pale skin. It was a haunting look.

I scanned the cabin to see what might have caused such a scream, but everything seemed perfectly in order. I turned my attention back to the tasks at hand; there was no room for error now. I had both everything to prove and everything to lose.

All was quiet for a few moments, but as we began to taxi down the runway, mournful cries erupted again.

"Allah! Allah!" General Jabbar shrieked. "Allah!"

What is going on? I wondered, as I looked back from my seat to the cabin. Again, nothing was amiss.

For the entire duration of our trip to Moscow, General Jabbar erupted into shouts, pleas, and cries every ten minutes or so. Every time, I jumped. It was nerve-racking.

The flight went smoothly until we began to make our initial descent into Moscow. At 400 feet, Major Awof reached over to disconnect the autopilot to begin manually guiding our descent.

But something was wrong. It wouldn't disconnect.

He tried again.

Nothing happened.

"The autopilot is not disengaging," he said tightly, but I already knew.

The ground was approaching fast, and my stomach knotted in fear. The Major was breathing hard, furiously attempting the disconnect. The ground was even closer now. It was time to take a more drastic approach.

"My God!" the Major shouted, as he used the joystick to execute a manual override of the autopilot. The entire plane began to shake. The knot in my belly twisted cruelly.

But we landed.

Safe and sound.

And I breathed a sigh of relief.

General Jabbar's business kept him in Moscow for several days. On the second night, the Russian ambassador invited everyone to dine with him at his home. I filed in quietly behind General Jabbar as the ambassador greeted everyone warmly.

The ambassador strode in my direction, grabbed my hand, and shook it firmly.

"Did something happen to you on your approach to Moscow?" he asked with a look of concern.

"No, no, sir. We landed just fine," I answered nervously.

"Hmm," the ambassador said.

"I spoke with the General, and he told me that something went wrong during your descent. He said that he believes the copilot made a mistake that caused the pilot to get angry and yell and the plane to shake."

Is that what he thought? That it was all my fault?

I wasn't sure what to say so I just stood there and smiled.

When it came time for the return flight, I took my position in the copilot seat again. Once again, General Jabbar boarded looking white as a sheet. But this time instead of throwing his haunted gaze to the heavens in fear, he watched me like a hawk, as if I was an omen of bad luck. As if I could single-handedly take down the entire flight.

My career on the VIP squad was off to a great start.

A few months later, I was tasked with flying General Jabbar again. By this time, I had made the all-important shift from the seat on the left to the seat on the right. I was the pilot now, a position that I proudly earned in record time.

I watched as General Jabbar approached the plane. Pale and stricken with fear. Just like last time. My squadron leader, Major Awof, walked beside him as he boarded the plane, which was customary.

"Hello, sir!" I said confidently from the captain's chair.

"Hello," General Jabbar said absently.

That is until General Jabbar's eyes met mine. Then he focused on me with laser-like precision and looked back toward Major Awof with great concern.

"Major Awof, how could you not find me an older pilot? Look at him, he's just a boy!" General Jabbar said.

It was obvious that General Jabbar remembered me—the culprit of the shaky landing in Moscow. We were not off to a good start.

"General Jabbar," Major Awof broke in, "do you know who this is? This is first flight lieutenant Mohammed. He's the son of General Adel Sulaiman. He's the best pilot we have on the squadron."

General Jabbar looked stunned for a minute as he scanned me up and down.

"You're General Adel's son?" he asked.

"Yes, sir. General Adel is my father, sir," I said proudly.

General Jabbar broke out in a wide smile.

"Well, if you're General Adel's son, that means you're good. You're good. Tell me, son, how is your father? Is he well?" General Jabbar asked.

In a matter of seconds, we went from being foes to friends.

"He is well, General. Thank you for asking."

"Tell your father I said hello, will you?" General Jabbar asked.

"Of course, sir, of course."

General Jabbar settled into his seat, still visibly anxious, but not nearly as much as he had been on the flight to Moscow.

This was my chance. I had found my way into General Jabbar's good graces, and I intended to stay there. This flight had to go perfectly.

And on that day, as luck would have it, it did go perfectly.

The takeoff was easy. The flight could have lulled a baby to sleep. And the landing was as smooth as a woman's leg fresh out of a bubble bath.

"Kiss the ground; don't fuck the ground"—that's what we always said.

I was proud.

More importantly, General Jabbar was impressed and happy.

On every flight General Jabbar took after that, he requested me by name. And so, the boy with the baby face had earned his keep on the VIP squad.

In those days, every single waking moment of my life revolved around being a pilot. When I wasn't flying, I was walking around the plane, reading about flights, talking with other pilots, or studying new planes. I even slept in the cockpit. I jumped at every opportunity to fly. I logged more flight hours than any other pilot in my position. This achievement wasn't born out of a competitive nature, but rather passion.

Flying was an art form to me, a love affair.

For my first two years on the VIP squad, I flew a whole variety of prominent and noteworthy people, from generals to ministers to dignitaries. Many of them began to request me by name, which made me feel proud and happy. I received generous monetary compensation as well as numerous gifts.

It seemed as though I was living the dream.

But the position was still grueling at times.

On April 17, 1988, the second Battle of Al-Faw, also known as the Operation Ramadan Mubarak or Blessed Ramadan, broke out. This battle would prove to be one of the major battles of the Iran–Iraq War.

Saddam ordered numerous chemical weapon bombardments, killing and sickening everyone nearby as well as the majority of the unprepared Iranian troops on the peninsula. I cannot speak with certainty on the number, but it is estimated that an amount of more than 100 tons of chemical agents were used. After this, the Republican Guard units launched their attack, moving down the peninsula twenty-one miles south of Umm Qasr. The Third Corps drove down the Faw peninsula while the Iraqi Special Forces moved through the marshy wetlands.

The Iraqi naval infantry also launched amphibious attacks onto the peninsula and landed behind Iranian defense lines. They quickly broke through the barbed-wire defensive barriers that the Iranians had erected. Though Iraq took some casualties clearing the minefields on the peninsula, we were able to capture the town of Faw just thirty-five hours into the attack.

The Iranians were completely taken by surprise and failed to launch an effective counterattack. They were outnumbered. Many, if not most, were killed or sickened by Iraqi mass chemical weapons. They kept up the fight at first, but soon began to retreat.

As the battle raged, my mission was to transport a variety of high-ranking military officials to various areas where they were needed to oversee the battle. I flew from Baghdad to Amman, Jordan, and picked up a high-ranking general and brought him back-to-back to Baghdad. As soon as I landed, I flew from Baghdad to Northern Iraq to get Chief of Staff and Iraqi General Nasser and bring him back to Baghdad. The wheels of the plane had barely kissed the earth before I was off again, flying a handful of high-ranking generals from Baghdad to Basra.

I didn't sleep and hardly ate or drank as the hours passed. I flew from Mosul to Basra. From Basra to Baghdad. From Baghdad to Basra. Flight after flight.

I didn't leave my seat for seventeen hours straight. The lack of food and water made bathroom breaks almost nonexistent. But I hardly noticed. There was an unmistakable thrill in the air that day. A successful liberation of the Al-Faw peninsula was something we had all longed for. Many of us were not aware of the means that Saddam had employed in the endeavor. We only knew an Iraqi territory would soon be free.

I remember one of the flights from Baghdad to Basra, which

is only about 500 kilometers or so from the Faw. It was 1:00 a.m. and the night sky enveloped the plane. My body was fatigued, but my mind was sharp, senses heightened.

Suddenly, the black sky exploded into shades of red, as if an angry painter had gone mad with brushstrokes. Even 100 kilometers from the battle, the sky told the story of the battle that raged on the ground below. It's an odd thing, you know, to see the colors of war from so high above, to hear the muffled sound of explosions in the distance, to know that a battle is raging below on earth while you sit and watch like a god in the sky. I sat there quietly, peacefully even, in my seat. The plane glided through the inky black sky as smooth as silk. Some perspectives almost make war beautiful.

It was an intense fight, but the peninsula was secured within thirty-five hours, with much of the captured Iranians' equipment still intact. We had hoped for the liberation of the Faw, and we'd gotten it. I felt elated, excited, and happy. I did not plan the battle or approve the method and means employed to achieve that victory. I was merely a soldier, carrying out orders, contributing my piece to the much larger puzzle at hand.

And then came a day that will forever be ingrained in my memory. It was a hot afternoon, as most are in Baghdad, and I set to preparing for the flight ahead. Oftentimes we didn't know who we would be flying until it was time for boarding. But we had a system of reference that sorted the VIPs into two groups: P1 and P2.

P1 included Saddam and members of the royal family such as his wife, children, or brothers. P2 covered everyone else from high-ranking military officials to dignitaries to ministers.

I didn't know who I would be flying on that day, only that it was a P1 flight. I expected it would be a member of the royal family.

Inside the reception area, I sat chatting with my squadron leader, waiting for my passengers to arrive. I noticed a black vehicle approaching. The passenger had arrived. But then came another black vehicle and then another. And another. And another. And then another. This much security could only mean one thing.

My heart leapt into my throat.

I am about to fly Saddam Hussein.

I am about to fly Saddam Hussein.

I am about to fly Saddam Hussein!

The words thudded in my mind to the sound of my sledgehammer heart. Panic washed over me.

I should already be in that plane. I need to get position before Saddam gets out of the vehicle.

I dropped my glass of water and nearly tripped over myself as I broke into a full-fledged run. All I could think about was getting to my seat before Saddam got out of the vehicle.

"Mohammed! Stop." The sound of my squadron leader's voice was sharp. "Mohammed, look at me right now and listen," he said. "You need to stop running and slow down. If you go sprinting up to that plane, security is going to think that something is wrong. And then they're going to shoot you. You can't act like this. Calm down. I'm not going to watch you get shot today just because you got too excited."

He was right.

Beating Saddam to the plane wasn't worth alarming security. They wouldn't think twice about dropping a young man with a bullet if they thought I was about to do something dangerous.

Breathe, breathe, breathe.

I threw my shoulders back and told myself to breathe as I calmly made my way to the plane.

As soon as I settled into my seat, my nerves began to dissipate. I was a pilot. And pilots don't have the luxury of giving into anxiety. I was trained to not allow stress to take control of my body. There was no room for sweaty palms, erratic maneuvers, or rough movements.

Saddam boarded the plane, along with his security team, and I glanced in his direction. There he was. The man I'd seen a hundred times on television screens and in newspapers. The man whose actions I hated with a passion. The man who held the power to end my life in a matter of moments if he so desired. All that pure evil contained inside the weathered skin, bones, and flesh of the man who was entering my plane. My jaw tightened with rising resentment. And then I forced it from my mind, laser focused on the task ahead. I inhaled and began to run through the pre-flight procedures, my movements slow and smooth.

The words of one of my instructors floated into my mind: "Treat this aircraft like you would treat a lady. With kindness, with tenderness. You must learn to know her inside and out, to guide her. Move slowly and with respect when you touch her. Don't grab her hard or she will break. Don't grab her too loosely or she will run away from you. Hold her gently but firmly."

Gently but firmly. Gently but firmly.

I repeated the words over and over to myself as I guided the plane for takeoff and navigated the flight to Mosul.

As I began the descent, I noticed that the other plane that held the remaining members of Saddam's security team had already landed.

They beat us. How in the world did they beat us?

Slow and steady. We're treating this lady slow and steady.

I can still remember my landing that day, smooth as silk. I remember sitting back, proud and satisfied.

I just flew Saddam Hussein.

I sat still and stoic as I waited for Saddam to exit the plane.

"Thank you, officer," Saddam Hussein said through the open doors of the cockpit.

Saddam Hussein is talking to you.

"Yes, sir." I nodded briefly in Saddam Hussein's direction, suddenly aware of every movement of my body.

No sudden movements. Make eye contact but not too much. Show respect but not fear.

My eyes locked with Saddam's. Those eyes never changed. Even when Saddam's face turned up into a smile, his eyes didn't follow. They were purposeful, unmoving, untouchable. Saddam paused for a moment when our eyes met.

"Well, you're very young, aren't you?" he said, taking in the youthful shape of my face.

Oh fuck. Again, with the young face thing.

"It was my pleasure and honor to fly you today, sir," I said.

"Thank you." The sound of my voice echoed as if spoken from the mouth of another. My heart pounded.

Saddam took a step closer. He reached out and placed his hand on my shoulder and held it there for a moment and then released with a squeeze of affection.

"Thank you," he said.

And then he was gone.

I watched Saddam's frame as he strode to a waiting vehicle, surrounded by security. I had just spoken with one of the most powerful and feared dictators in the entire world. I could still feel the warmth of Saddam's hand on my shoulder, and his words echoed in my ear. The man who had killed my best childhood friend. The bloodthirsty dictator who loved war and led our nation into it without regard for the loss of human life. The tyrant who ruled with fear and cruelty.

Saddam sent me a gift equivalent to nearly $3,000 US dollars that day. There was a reason every pilot in Iraq wanted to be on the VIP squad. And I was grateful for the money.

I still hated Saddam with every fiber of my being. But I swallowed my feelings. I was a pilot. To me that was not just a job; it was an identity. It didn't matter to me whether I was flying Saddam or flying a monkey.

And so, I flew with honor and with pride that day.

CHAPTER THREE_

Let me begin by saying that I am not a superstitious man.

I do not believe in bad omens or signs or curses. This is a good thing when you're a pilot. You cannot afford to give credence to premonitions and act accordingly, or you may find yourself fulfilling a prophecy that had no merit in the first place.

But if I were a superstitious man, if I believed in miracles and curses and wanted to prove my theories correct, then there is one day I would remember as irrefutable proof that bad omens exist.

One morning in the summer of 1987, I blinked my eyes open from sleep, making no move to get up immediately. When a long day of flying lies ahead, those few quiet morning moments are valuable. One breath, two breaths. Then my feet hit the floor.

And so it begins.

I ate, dressed, gathered my things, and kissed my children—Rania, Rula, and Baby Rand, who had just recently been born. I left my home early, allowing myself ample time to check over the aircraft and prepare for the flight.

"Hello, Mohammed!" said a voice, greeting me just as I settled into the front seat of my car.

Shit. I know that voice.

I turned to see my neighbor standing not far, watering his plants. My neighbor's wife was beside him, and she waved too.

"Hello, Mohammed!" she said.

There was something dark and disturbing about the way they stood there and looked at me. I shivered a bit and tried to shake the crawling feeling that spread through my body as I looked at them. They were proven to be rude, horrible, and mean people. The man was a tyrant, and his wife was something of a witch. They watched me with a knowing look, grinning with a hint of evil.

"Good morning," I said as quickly as possible, hardly making eye contact. Uneasiness festered in my belly as I drove away.

Fuck.

I didn't have a good feeling about the day.

Be safe today. Make no move without carefully thinking it over.

I promised myself to take extra care with my preflight procedures, to check over every single detail. If something was wrong, I'd find it. I arrived at the airport a few hours later and began running through procedures to prepare for the flight, which would be lengthy. I was scheduled to fly the Minister of Commerce from Baghdad to Sanaa, Yemen; and then from Sanaa to Aden, which was also in Yemen; then from Aden to Djibouti; and from Djibouti to Mogadishu, Somalia.

I checked the aircraft, the maps, and the communication systems. I checked to make sure we had received permission for landing in each country we planned to make a stop at.

Everything looked perfect.

But the gnawing feeling in my belly continued.

I gathered the two large books that I always brought along with me on each flight, filled with maps, route and approaching charts, and other necessary flight information. Then I checked the navigation system once and then checked it again.

For two hours I walked, looked, checked, and double checked. This was my custom before long flights, but I felt an increased sense of urgency that particular day.

Everything looked perfect.

At 10:30 a.m., the Minister arrived and boarded the plane.

"Good morning, sir," I said brightly. "How are you?"

"Very good, very good," he said as he made his way into the cabin and settled in for the long flight.

I started the engines. Ironically, it was protocol to start with the second engine and end with the first engine.

Engine number 2—*normal and ready.*

Engine number 3—*normal and ready.*

Engine number 4—*normal and ready.*

Engine number 1—*normal and ready.*

Because of the long flight, the aircraft was heavy with fuel, which meant takeoff would be different. I couldn't risk eating the runway due to the heaviness of the craft, which meant that instead of gradually gathering speed and power as I would normally do during takeoff, I put the brake on and applied full power. I checked everything from pressure to temperature.

All good.

I released the brake.

Climbing. Climbing. Climbing.

We were airborne and twenty minutes later, we had reached 27,000 feet. Smooth as silk.

BOOM!

An explosive sound filled the air, and my whole body jolted. Panic coursed through me like an electric shock.

Something was wrong.

Very wrong.

The cockpit roared with noise. The entire panel before me blinked neon red.

Beep. Beep. Beep.

The sounds matched my rapid heart rate.

Fire in engine 2.

In the chaos, my mind processed the information before me, and my hands responded mechanically.

"You handle communications, and I'll handle the drills!" I shouted to my copilot, or P2, over the noise.

He already knew the protocol.

"Mayday, Mayday!" he yelled.

We waited for an answer; every second was an eternity.

"Mayday, Mayday, Mayday!" he yelled again, along with

our flight number and call sign. "We have engine fire, I repeat, we have engine fire."

Finally, a voice crackled over the radio in response. Now that our message had been received, we would be given priority on all communications and routing to the air base as we attempted to land.

Simultaneously, I began to go through the procedures I had practiced a hundred times in flight school.

This is real. This is not a drill.

Fuel, air, and an ignition source, or heat, are the three ingredients a fire needs, and, unfortunately, a running aircraft has plenty of hot things that can quickly ignite.

I needed to cut off the oxygen to prevent fumes from blowing into the cabin. The oxygen was feeding the fire and air flowing through the vents would only help the fire grow.

Immediately, I cut off the bleed air system, which uses a network of ducts, valves, and regulators to conduct medium- to high-pressure air to various locations within the aircraft, such as the air-conditioning packs where it is filtered and then cooled using an expansion process.

I continued to run through the protocols and procedures as my P2 shouted over the radio.

"What's happening, what's happening? Is everything okay?" The Minister's voice sounded into the cockpit. He steadied himself in the doorway, shaking with alarm. He was yellow as if every drop of blood in his body had descended to his feet.

"Everything is okay, sir. We have it under control," I said, trying to sound calm. "Please return to your seat and remain seated, sir."

And for the moment, we did have things under control. The fire appeared to be contained and we prepared to make an emergency landing.

But then another thought hit me with force:

We have 8,000 pounds of fuel still in the tank.

This presented a whole new set of challenges. The higher mass would require a higher approach and touchdown speed. We would be at high risk of overshooting the runway or overheating the brakes, which would result in brake failure and, once again, overshooting the runway.

I needed to dump the fuel.

There are several scenarios in which fuel dumping is a bad idea. One of those is when experiencing an engine fire. Another is when flying over a city.

We had an engine fire, *and* we were flying over a city.

"I'm going to jettison the fuel," I said, turning to my P2.

The P2 looked at me as though I was crazy. "With a fire in the engine?"

"We have to," I said. "Even the risk of dumping fuel was better than trying to land weighed down with 8,000 pounds of fuel."

We had entered the circling zone, only a few minutes away from the Baghdad airfield where we would be making our emergency landing.

I radioed into control: "Sir, I am going to attempt to jettison some of our additional fuel. Keep eyes on the aircraft, will you? Let me know if you see flames or smoke."

"Roger that. I got eyes on you now."

I pushed the button to begin the fuel dump.

"Are we still looking okay?" I asked.

"Everything looks good so far. I'll keep my eyes on you the entire time. I've got you," he assured me.

"If you see black smoke, I need to know immediately," I said.

"So far you're looking okay," he said. "I've alerted the ground to your situation, and they are preparing for your landing."

I knew what that meant.

The fire teams. Trucks. Emergency vehicles.

They were preparing for us to crash.

My heart thudded. My hands moved mechanically. Thoughts of my brother came to my mind.

Today is not my day to die.

We were now just over the center of Bagdad, and I turned the plane toward the airfield. A trail of white smoke billowed behind the aircraft.

At least it's not black.

The fuel dump continued.

Now we were only 1,500 feet above the city center. I could see the green trees of the park below. I knew the fuel was touching the ground.

But we had no other alternatives.

The ground was getting closer and closer.

It was time to land.

I stopped the fuel jettison at the last possible minute. Even with the fuel we'd eliminated, I knew we were still overweight.

I have to make this landing.

As a pilot there are a handful of moments that you truly feel the power that comes with flying a plane. When you understand the responsibility wielded within your two hands. When you grasp the gravity that lies in every movement, every twitch of your fingers, every decision you make.

No one is coming to do it for you. It's just you. Your hands. Your mind. Your decisions.

Suddenly, a sense of crystal clarity washed over me. My hands and my mind were no longer mine but a part of the aircraft.

Tethered.

Connected.

One.

Down, down, down. Wheels and earth connected.

Another breath.

And another.

We are okay.

Flashing fire trucks, emergency vehicles, and first responders surrounded us and sprang into action. The minister was evacuated from the plane immediately. A team of engineers took over and began to inspect the black engine which was covered in soot. I took a deep breath.

We made it.

But I had little time to gather my thoughts. Within half an hour, another aircraft had been prepared, and I was once again walking to it with my things. The Minister was under orders from Saddam to make this meeting, which meant that under no circumstances would the meeting be postponed or rescheduled. There was no time to catch our breath, no chance of asking for an extra hour to collect ourselves after a near-death experience. We had to keep moving.

I conducted my preflight checks and procedures as carefully as possible for about fifty minutes, and everything looked good. The Minister boarded looking absolutely petrified, and it was time to take off again, not even two hours after landing in a smoking plane.

My hands glided over the instruments as I engaged for takeoff, and I willed myself not to give into anxious thoughts.

I am a pilot. It's who I am; it's in my blood.

I did not surrender to racing thoughts, and I didn't second guess myself. I couldn't. I knew that succumbing to the vortex of anxiety and doubts would prove to be more dangerous than the fire.

It is in times like these that you must believe that *you are a pilot*. You must believe that it's in your blood, that you have instincts within you that can be relied upon, like breathing.

So, I moved with intuition and certainty, like a dance. The aircraft became an extension of my mind and body, and soon we were airborne once again.

Once I reached cruising altitude, my mind had a chance to reflect on the events of the day. And then suddenly I realized: *It's because you saw those damn unlucky, horrible neighbors today. That's bad luck if I've ever seen it.*

As I said before, I am not a superstitious man. But if I was, I would have found the source of this cursed day and would have known the cause with certainty. I told myself there could only be so many unlucky mishaps in one day. This day had already taken more than its portion, right?

The flight went smoothly, and we landed in Sanaa, Yemen. The Minister conducted his business quickly, and within a few hours we were off again, this time to Aden, which was also in Yemen. The flight was short, which meant I had no need to refuel. We were making excellent time, despite how the day had started. Once the Minister finished his business in Aden, we flew to Djibouti, another quick flight, and landed by sunset.

Once we landed in Djibouti, a car was waiting to transport us to the coast where we'd stay for the night. I was grateful for the respite, knowing we had a long flight awaiting us in the morning. By 8:00 a.m. I began preparing for the long flight to Mogadishu, Somalia.

The plane had only 4,000 pounds of fuel left from our travels the day before and I made sure it was properly refueled and equipped with 10,000 pounds inside the wings. Based upon my calculations, this gave us more than enough fuel to not only reach Mogadishu, but to make any necessary diversions for emergency landings should the need arise. It's imperative that you consider every possibility as a pilot; you must hope for the best but prepare for the worst.

By 11:00 a.m. we were off.

The flight began smoothly, and soon we were cruising gently through the air. We crossed outside of the Djibouti control zone, and I knew it would still be a while before I'd be able to establish contact with Mogadishu, not only because of the distance but also due to the fact that the Mogadishu control center had only very rudimentary equipment.

So we flew in silence over the thick African jungle as I waited to get close enough to establish contact. We flew over dense jungles with absolutely no place for a crash landing, notorious for being inhabited by cannibals and witches. Knowing this, I took care in strategizing and calculating a backup plan before takeoff in the case something should go wrong.

In every flight, there is a point at which an aircraft is no longer capable of returning to the airfield from which it took off due to fuel considerations. Once you've passed this point the aircraft must proceed to some other destination.

I checked the navigation system. It was time to attempt to establish communication with Mogadishu.

"Mogadishu, this is Iraqi flight number 866 from Djibouti. We are about seventy minutes from Djibouti and about ninety minutes from Mogadishu. Do you copy?" I said.

No answer.

I knew their communication system wasn't the most reliable or well equipped, so the silence did not come as a concern.

Ten minutes later I radioed in again.

"Mogadishu, this is Iraqi flight number 866 from Djibouti. We are about eighty minutes from Djibouti and now about eighty minutes from Mogadishu. Do you copy?" I said.

No answer.

I waited another ten minutes and radioed in again.

"Mogadishu, this is Iraqi flight number 866 from Djibouti.

We are about ninety minutes from Djibouti and about seventy minutes from Mogadishu. Do you copy?" I said.

No answer.

Every ten minutes, I attempted to establish contact with Mogadishu but still received no answer. A deep uneasiness spread through me as I sat in silence.

Why aren't they answering?

I radioed another time and was again greeted with silence.

It's just a problem with communications.

We were quickly approaching critical point, or CP, a time which occurs at the moment when flight time to destination and the flight time back to base are the same.

While I had not been able to establish communication yet, I also didn't have any reason to draw the conclusion that something was wrong. If I turned back and the Minister missed the scheduled meetings with the Somali government officials and it turned out to be a simple communication problem, then I would be in no small amount of trouble. I had worked hard to establish myself as one of the most reliable and requested pilots on the VIP squad. I couldn't ruin that reputation or risk the dire consequences that would come from unnecessarily turning back.

Not long after passing CP, we approached the Point of No Return, or *PNR*. I still had been unable to establish communication, but at this point, I didn't feel that it should be a cause for alarm considering the distance we were from Mogadishu and the state of their equipment.

And so, I made the decision to continue.

Past Critical Point.

Past the Point of No Return.

We were committed now. No matter what happened, we would be landing in Mogadishu. If the engine caught fire, if there was an emergency on board, if there was an explosion, Mogadishu was where we would be landing. There were no other viable options at this point.

We entered Mogadishu airspace.

Surely we'll establish communication now that we're close.

"Mogadishu, this is Iraqi flight number 866 from Djibouti. We are making our approach, about twenty minutes out. Do you copy?" I said.

I then waited for some sound, some response to set my knotted stomach at ease.

But there was only silence and no relief for my mounting fear.

I willed myself to wait for sixty seconds, to get a little closer, wait a little longer.

It felt like an eternity.

I picked up the radio again and forced my voice to sound confident and casual as I tried to establish communication, if for nothing else than to calm my own nerves. But when I was met with a wall of silence again, the forced calm of my tone did nothing to bring a sense of peace. I changed the frequency and tried again.

Still no answer.

I could hear communication between other aircrafts, but there was nothing from Mogadishu.

There has to be something wrong with my communications system.

It seemed like the only logical explanation for the situation.

It was time to begin the descent, and I had no choice but to simply proceed as normal. Now that we were in close range to the airport, I flipped through the pages of my reference books, found the frequency of the local control tower, and switched the radio to try and communicate directly with them instead of the control center.

This has got to work.

"Mogadishu, this is Iraqi flight number 866 from Djibouti. We are approaching fast. Do you copy?" I said.

Still no answer.

Uneasiness morphed into alarm. Something was obviously wrong, and the luxury of time to wait for a response was not on my side. But, as with everything in flight, there is a procedure, and I began the procedure for communications failure.

I made a low approach and rocked the wing of the plane back and forth. Right to left, right to left, right to left, down the entire runway. This was the signal that the communications system was down. They'd have to be blind not to see the sign.

I then returned downwind and prepared to make a normal approach and landing.

Where's the flare?

My eyes were trained on the control tower, waiting to see a flare go up, the sign that they had received my signal.

Red flare if it wasn't safe to land; green if it was.

Nothing. Everything was eerily quiet.

Let's try this again.

Once again, I made a low approach and rocked the wing of the plane back and forth. Right to left, right to left, right to left, down the entire runway. Again, I returned downwind and prepared to make a normal approach and landing.

I looked for a flare, a sign of movement, *anything*. But there was nothing. Not even cars in the parking lot or service cars on the field.

The entire field was totally deserted.

"What are we going to do?" my P2 asked.

"Oh, we're going to land this fucker," I said. We didn't have enough fuel to go anywhere else or to stay in the air for that much longer. Our only option was to land.

Here we go.

Down, down, down.

My body felt the contact of the runway as if the wheels of the plane were connected to me. As the plane slowed, I felt a mixture of relief and continued uneasiness. We were on the ground, safe and in one piece. That was the good news. The bad news was that we were in an airport in Somalia that appeared to be completely deserted, a notion which was more than a little disconcerting.

The runway was so small that I had to backtrack the plane after landing to the designated area. I looked for any sign of movement or life.

Still nothing.

What the hell is going on here?

There was an eerie hush across the entire airfield as I began the process of shutting down the plane. The Minister exited the aircraft just as two vehicles approached in the distance.

Finally, some human contact.

Six men exited the vehicles and approached, looking concerned.

"What in the world are you doing here? Why did you come right now?" The voice of one of the men reached me in the cockpit, and I stood and moved closer to hear more.

The Minister explained the nature of his business to the man but was quickly interrupted.

"No, no, no. This is not a good time. Haven't you heard?" He looked at us like we were crazy.

"Heard what?" the Minister asked.

"There's been a military coup in the capital. The entire city is in chaos. They've got machine guns and weapons. It's not safe to be here right now."

Suddenly it all made sense. The lack of communication, the deserted airport.

What are the odds of us landing in Somalia in the middle of a military coup d'état?

This was the first thought that struck me.

And then...

Those damn neighbors and their bad luck.

"Mohammed, can we get back in the plane and turn back for Djibouti?" the Minister asked.

I met his eyes.

"No, sir, we are going to need a significant amount of fuel before we can go anywhere," I said.

"How did this happen? How did we not know what was going on?" the Minister asked, looking at me.

I explained the situation, the lack of communication, and the decision I made at the Point of No Return.

There are a thousand decisions you make as a pilot, and the weight of responsibility is never more apparent than when you are questioned about one of those choices. I did my best to convey my point of view. But the Minister seemed only focused on what we were going to do to get out of this situation.

"Come with us," the man said to the Minister. "We'll escort you to the embassy where you'll be safe until you can leave."

The Minister nodded, and another man stepped forward to open the door and help load the Minister's things into the vehicle. It was the only option at this point.

I continued standing by the plane.

"Mohammed, come," the Minister said. "It's not safe here. You need to be at the embassy."

But I made no move to come with him.

"No, sir," I said, meeting the Minister's eyes. "With all due respect, I can't leave my plane. If things are as bad as they say, there's no telling what they might do to it. I need to stay here."

The Minister scanned my face as if trying to decide if he should attempt to convince me further. But my eyes were set, and my expression was resolute. I was going to stay with my plane, and over my dead body was anyone going to cause it harm.

The Minister nodded briefly. He understood.

"I'll stay with him," one of the men offered, moving to stand beside me as the Minister loaded his things and ducked inside the vehicle.

"Thank you," I breathed, happy to have an ally. I didn't know what I was going to be up against in the next few hours.

The vehicles left for the embassy, and I walked around the

plane, trying to make myself busy. I tensed at the sound of gunshots in the distance. Machine-gun fire, then small explosives.

What if they come here?

After about twenty minutes, another vehicle approached, and a Somalia man exited and strode toward the plane.

"Hello, hello," he said. "I'm sure you have heard and understand that there has been a military coup against the president, and the situation is very dangerous."

I nodded.

"I understand," I said. "I just need fuel for my plane, and then we will be on our way."

"Oh fuel, fuel, fuel," the man said, shaking his head back and forth. "This may be very hard to get, my friend. But I will try."

I told him what kind of fuel was needed, and the Somalia man promised to do everything he could to get it for me.

"Give me time. Just give me time," he said and rode off again.

There was nothing I could do but wait. Here we were, stranded in Somalia in the middle of a military coup, without enough fuel to get home, and all I could do was be still, wait, and listen to the sound of gunshots in the distance.

After a little while, the man returned, looking pleased.

"I found the fuel you are looking for, sir! We have it," he said.

Relief swept through me.

"Can I see it?" I asked, trying not to take on false hope.

"Yes, sir, follow me."

We walked together to where the fuel was stored, and sure enough it was the right kind.

But there was a problem.

The fuel was stored in small barrels atop wooden pallets. These were not the massive storage containers with large hoses to rapidly siphon the fuel like I was accustomed to, which could easily deliver 10,000 pounds of fuel in a relatively short period of time.

These were barrels. Small barrels that would have to be transported on the wooden pallets with a forklift to the aircraft and then manually pumped into the plane.

This is going to take forever.

But it was our only way out.

And so, we began.

The hot, humid air pressed down on me as sweat poured from my temples. Progress was painstakingly slow. The sound of machine-gun fire tearing through the air sent a panic through me. I desperately wanted to hurry, to find a way to make a fast escape. But there was no way to expedite the process.

Barrel after barrel.

Hour after hour.

Bead of sweat after bead of sweat.

There was nothing to relieve the agony of the slow process.

After eight hours of manually refueling the aircraft, we almost had enough. I asked the man from the embassy who had stayed behind with me to send word to the Minister that it was almost time to leave. He agreed and began the drive to the embassy as communications were down for the entire city. I hoped they would make it back safely.

When the last barrel had been pumped into the aircraft, I could have shouted. I conducted pre-flight procedures and mentally began to plan my takeoff strategy to avoid being shot down.

The Minister arrived and boarded the plane in a rush. I took my seat and took a deep breath.

It's time.

I engaged the engine. Full speed down the runway.

Under normal circumstances, I would have turned right and passed over the city to get positioned in the direction of Saudi Arabia, our next destination. But I couldn't risk flying over the city and being shot down during takeoff. As soon as we were airborne, I stayed low and then cut left over the water. Once over the water, I started climbing fast.

10,000 feet.

15,000 feet.

20,000 feet.

"Can't get me now," I whispered as we flew safely over the city.

I'm not sure I have ever been so relieved to be airborne.

The flight to Saudi Arabia went smoothly, and in the quiet of the cockpit, my mind replayed the events of the last two days.

An engine fire, an emergency landing, a flight with no communication, landing in Somalia in the middle of a military coup, manually refueling a plane—it was hard to believe that so much had happened in such a short amount of time.

As I sat in silence, I felt keenly aware of the delicate balance between life and death, between things turning out good and things going very, very badly. I thought of the hundreds of large and small decisions I had made that could have altered the course of life had I not made the right call.

I thought of every aircraft maneuver made by my hands and what could have been different had I allowed panic to overtake me.

I felt myself breathe in and out.

I felt grateful.

Once we were safely on the ground, the Minister's security team informed me that he would be taking some extra time to visit Mecca, which was located just an hour away, to pray and give thanks to God for sparing his life twice over the course of the past two days.

"Will you be joining us?" a member of the security team asked.

"Not this time," I said. "I'm going to do a little shopping."

Because, as I said, I am not a religious man or a superstitious man, and I didn't feel the need to pray.

And I am never talking to those damn next-door neighbors again.

CHAPTER FOUR_

There were many things about being a pilot on the VIP squad that made life interesting. The money was incredible. The gifts I received were generous. The ability to see all kinds of exotic destinations made the job exciting. But there was never a moment when I could escape from the truth that I worked for one of the most ruthless and brutal dictators the world has ever known. Sure, there were days and weeks, even months when I could distract myself from this knowledge.

The generous sums of money I received, as well as the prestige and honor of the position, certainly helped with that distraction. And this was by design. They knew just how to incentivize us and keep us loyal. Almost all of us on the VIP squad had families to provide for and futures to build. Being a VIP pilot opened doors we hadn't dreamed of. It gave us money to build homes and give our children gifts that made their faces light up. And once we tasted that good life, none of us wanted to give it up.

Even still, there was an underlying sense of fear that I couldn't shake. A feeling like always walking a tightrope. To make a mistake wasn't a matter of getting called into an office and reprimanded. It was a matter of life and death. If I made a powerful man angry or did anything that made it look like I had something to hide, my head and the heads of my family were on the line. I couldn't say the wrong things; I couldn't lean too far this way or that. My life was at the mercy of the moods, impressions, and impulses of a volatile dictator and the unpredictable characters he surrounded himself with.

Living under this kind of pressure is hard to describe. It's something I wouldn't wish upon anyone. Even on the good days, and there were good days, I couldn't let my guard down. I couldn't fully relax. I couldn't speak my mind without first looking around to see who was listening. Every behavior, every word spoken, every decision made was calculated. Like the tightrope walker whose face beads with sweat at the sheer exertion of just staying balanced, just keeping still, just forcing every part of yourself into perfect submission to avoid a great fall.

But it was all I knew. And so, in many ways, I didn't even notice. I didn't feel the exhaustion of it. I didn't fight it. I just learned the walk, learned the dance, learned the art of strategic control. I learned to suppress my feelings, hide my opinions, quiet my voice, control my behavior. Perhaps if you are born into freedom and accustomed to saying what you think and doing what you want, the idea of this controlled existence seems like a straitjacket, like a great injustice. But when you are born into it, when all you know is the art of suppressing your own voice, thoughts, and opinions, and it seems normal somehow. When all you've ever known is the confines of a straitjacket, you don't feel the suffocating tightness that closes in. You learn to surrender, learn to keep silent, learn to control yourself. You learn to walk the tightrope. And after a while, it's all so habitual that you hardly notice.

I calculated my words each time I spoke in public, never voicing my true feelings about Saddam Hussein and the men who led our country. Still, the feelings rose and bubbled up in me, like a shaken can of soda, just waiting for the lid to blow. But I controlled myself. I put a smile on my face and treated everyone who boarded my aircraft with the same dignity, respect, and kindness that I would give my grandmother. And I focused all my energy into being the best pilot possible. But a small handful of times the pressure of it all was almost too much to contain, and the can of soda almost popped open.

Two of these moments came at the hands of the same man, Sabawi Ibrahim al-Tikriti, Saddam's half-brother. Saddam employed many family members and appointed them to positions of power. But the dynamics and history of his flesh and blood is both complicated and sad. Saddam Hussein's brother and father died of cancer before his birth. It is rumored that these deaths took a great toll on the mental health of Saddam's mother, Subha Tulfah al-Mussallat, who became so depressed that she attempted to abort the pregnancy and commit suicide. When she finally did birth Saddam, there were many reports that she refused to have anything to do with him and left his care to his uncle for the first several years of his life.

After a while, however, Saddam's mother remarried, and Saddam gained three half-brothers. His stepfather, Ibrahim al-Hassan, treated Saddam harshly and brutally abused him, both physically and psychologically. At about age ten, Saddam fled the family and returned to live in Baghdad with his uncle Khairallah Talfah, who became a fatherly figure to Saddam. He maintained a relationship with his half-brothers throughout his life, and after his rise to power, he placed them in leadership positions within the government.

I flew many of these family members on multiple occasions. But there was one man that proved to be the most challenging out of everyone. And that was Sabawi Ibrahim al-Tikriti. Sabawi was the leader of the Iraqi secret service, or the *Mukhabarat*, the head of the Directorate of General Security, and a presidential advisor to Hussein.

On one particular day, I received an order from the operation center to prepare an aircraft. I would be flying someone from the P2 category, which meant a high-level government or military official such as a minister or general. P1 was reserved for Saddam and his immediate family only, and P3 was for other members of small, local delegations such as the Iraqi Air Force or Army. My instructions were to prepare to fly to Amarah, Iraq, a town south of Baghdad.

I prepared the aircraft without much thought as to who I'd be flying. After being on the VIP squad for several years, I had met just about every high-level government and military official, even Saddam himself, and the initial nervous thrill of wondering who would be in my aircraft had dwindled over time.

But when I received word that I'd be flying Sabawi, the pit of my stomach knotted. Sabawi was notorious for being angry, unpredictable, and volatile. I had heard reports from my colleagues of Sabawi's mood swings, insanity, and dangerous behaviors. My chest constricted as I prepared myself for walking the tightrope of perfect behavior. No sideways glances, no erratic movements, nothing that could possibly attract Sabawi's rage.

After preparing the aircraft, I called a friend of mine who was in Amarah, our destination, to check on the weather. I wanted to be prepared for everything.

"It's not good, Mohammed," my friend said. "A sandstorm just blew in, and we've got zero visibility. I'm afraid there can be no takeoff or landing here until it passes."

After hanging up, I looked over the weather report and immediately knew I had a problem on my hands. A sandstorm would make it nearly impossible to fly there. Additionally, the airport where we were scheduled to land was small and ill-equipped with navigation technology, only increasing the risk factor of attempting to land there in the middle of a storm. But the idea of telling Sabawi that I wouldn't be able to fly him almost scared me more than the sandstorm. I set to making last-minute preparations to the aircraft and hoped with everything in me that the storm would somehow clear before Sabawi arrived.

But before long, a row of vehicles pulled into the airfield and out strode the man himself. Everything about Sabawi made me uneasy, and my skin pricked with awareness. As Sabawi drew near and our eyes locked, the knot in my belly tightened. There was something rabid in Sabawi's eyes, as if a wild form of evil lay just behind them. His face was weathered and drawn like the shell of a human whose soul and conscience had been long ago seared. He boarded the plane, along with a security team of seven.

"Hello," Sabawi said, throwing the word in my direction with disdain as he passed by the cockpit. As if I should count myself lucky to even be acknowledged by him. I swallowed. The weather conditions still hadn't changed, and it was up to me to inform Sabawi.

"Sir, good afternoon. I hope you are well," I said. The fear in my belly created a perfect, smooth politeness in my voice. "I regret to inform you there is a sandstorm in Amarah right now, making the conditions unsafe for flight. We will need to wait until it has passed before takeoff."

I held my breath as I waited for Sabawi's response, searching for some hint of reaction in his cold, lifeless eyes.

Sabawi didn't say anything and walked to his seat and settled in. I remained in the cockpit, hoping with everything in me that the sandstorm gods would take pity on me and calm the storm.

After waiting a few minutes, a member of Sabawi's team approached the cockpit.

"Mr. Sabawi wishes me to ask you why we are still waiting. Why have we not taken off?"

I cleared my throat again.

"Please inform Mr. Sabawi that, unfortunately, there is a

sandstorm in Amarah, making it unsafe for us to land there at this time. We will take off as soon as it is safe," I said.

The man nodded slightly and turned around to relay the message to Sabawi. But within a matter of moments, he was back.

"Mr. Sabawi would like a word with you," he said.

With a twisted stomach and sweaty hands, I followed the man to where Sabawi sat.

Those terrible eyes trained on me with a look of rising rage. But his voice was unsettlingly calm and calculated when he spoke.

"You say there is bad weather, do you?" Sabawi said. He asked the question as if I were a kindergartener. "What weather?" His voice rose sharply as his hand pointed to the window next to him where the bright sun shone into clear skies. "What bad weather do you speak of?"

Before I even opened my mouth, I knew I was at the mercy of an unreasonable man. I already knew that nothing I could say would satisfy him.

"Sir, it's the weather conditions in Amarah. There is a sandstorm and, unfortunately, we cannot land until it clears. They've even closed the airport, sir," I said.

Sabawi's eyes twitched with escalating rage at each word I spoke.

"Look!" Sabawi screamed. "Look to the sky! I can see Allah over there. That is how clear the skies are. I see no storm. Are you just scared to fly?"

Before I could even manage the words, Sabawi's voice rose yet again.

"GO!" He waved his hand at me as if he were shooing away a dog. "GO FLY THIS FUCKING PLANE!"

The untamed fury in Sabawi's words and the coldness in his eyes told me everything I needed to know. It would be better to attempt to fly in a sandstorm than to cross him. It was almost as if he was daring me, as if he would be happy to have some excuse to relieve his anger by seeing my body drop on the spot.

I had no choice.

"Yes, sir," I said and walked to the cockpit, my heart thudding like a sledgehammer.

Maybe by some stroke of luck the sandstorm will clear before we arrive.

It was the only thing I could hope for.

I returned dutifully to my seat.

Anger boiled within me. I was a pilot. And a damn good one. I was trained to consider the safety of my passengers, of my aircraft above all else. I was trained to make the right call in these types of situations. But now my hands were tied. I was knowingly driving into a sandstorm against my better judgment because of a crazy man. The fear of him was greater than that of the storm. I felt powerless.

"What's the matter?" my copilot asked. He hadn't heard the conversation.

"Don't talk," I said brusquely, afraid that if I spoke the anger inside of me would flow and never stop. "Let's just go."

So I took off. Even while everything in me screamed that I was doing the wrong thing, that I was making a mistake.

Takeoff was smooth, and we cruised uneventfully for a little while through the clear skies over Baghdad and just beyond.

I knew that would soon change.

Just fifty miles outside of Baghdad, the entire horizon became nothing but a blanket of dust. Even at 18,000 feet I could see it—sand like a thick duvet cover encompassing the entire world below it.

I grimaced.

Everything in me wanted to turn back. These were no conditions to fly, and it was only going to get worse. But the thought of those cold, rage-filled eyes and the sound of that crazed scream was enough to keep me glued to my seat. I continued on.

The sky grew darker. About forty miles outside of Amarah, I began to make the descent, as if everything was normal, as if the sky was clear and the sun was shining instead of swirling with grit.

Within minutes, the entire aircraft was encompassed by swirling sand as if we had taken a plunge into the ground itself. It surrounded us on every side, painting us with sand so thick that it looked like mud. I couldn't see anything. But still I continued. If I was going to die, it wasn't to be at the hands of a crazy man on a bad day.

This type of flight is referred to as an IMC situation, or Instrument Meteorological Conditions. This is a flight category that describes weather conditions that require the pilot to fly primarily by reference to instruments rather than by outside visual references.

I continued to descend, and the dust only grew more

suffocating, pressing in on every side. At 1,500 feet I was engaged in full IMC mode. The term *flying blind* takes on a sadistic twist when someone is actually faced with it. My mind went into a state of total clarity as I followed every bad weather procedure with clinical precision.

1,200 feet.

Land in a sandstorm or face Sabawi's wrath?

900 feet.

Sandstorm or wrath?

600 feet.

Sandstorm or wrath?

I couldn't do it. Every instinct inside of me just wouldn't allow it. It was crazy. It was dangerous. How could I risk the safety of the aircraft and every life inside of that plane because of the insanity of one man?

I'd try again.

I climbed to 1,500 feet and circled the aircraft for another descent. Landing gear in position.

1,200 feet.

Land in a sandstorm or face Sabawi's wrath?

900 feet.

Sandstorm or wrath?

600 feet.

Sandstorm or wrath?

500 feet.

I can't do this.

I climbed up to 1,500 feet again.

I turned to my copilot and said, "Go and tell Sabawi that I regret to inform him that we cannot land until the storm clears.

For his safety, as well as that of everyone aboard, we will be returning to Baghdad."

My copilot nodded and stood up.

I steadied my breath as I waited for my copilot to return, hoping that even a man as crazy as Sabawi could see the storm.

Please let it be enough that I tried. Please let it be enough.

"What did he say?" I asked my copilot when he returned almost as quickly as he left.

"He didn't say a damn thing," the copilot said. "Not a damn thing."

I had to hope that the silence was the concession of a proud man, not the space needed to harness anger into a plan for retaliation.

This landing has to be perfect.

And it was. Smooth as silk.

Kissing the ground, not fucking it.

Perfection.

Once on the ground, the gnawing sense of uneasiness returned. I had no idea what state Sabawi would be in, and I dreaded facing him.

Had the flight given him time to simmer down or boil up further? Would he understand my decision or have my head on a platter?

I could hear footsteps behind him as Sabawi made his way through the plane to exit.

Closer, closer, closer.

I steeled myself for what would come next.

But nothing did. Sabawi left without a single word.

I breathed in a lungful of air the moment the vehicle door shut behind Sabawi and he drove away.

Rage billowed within me. I hated feeling so powerless and so patronized. I hated that I had just been forced to do something dangerous because of one man's moronic reasoning. How could I be expected to pilot an aircraft with my hands tied behind my back, with my ability to make the right decisions completely stripped away from me?

"Everything okay?" my squadron leader asked as I brushed past him, my face focused and drawn.

The questions were enough to make a crack in the dam I had erected around my feelings. I spun around to face my squadron leader and stood eye-to-eye, passion and anger spilling from every part of me.

"No. No, I am not okay. And you want to know why? Sabawi. That man is crazy. Not only crazy, but also stupid and insane. He wants to get into my aircraft and dictate how I fly. He doesn't understand safety protocols, he doesn't understand weather patterns, he doesn't understand a damn thing, and yet that son of a bitch made me fly in a FUCKING SANDSTORM," I said "I told him it was unsafe, and I told him we needed to wait. But he wouldn't take no for an answer, and we all know the stories about Sabawi. You don't cross him. How the hell am I expected to be a pilot like this?"

A flood of pent-up anger spewed onto my squadron leader, but he didn't flinch. I could see the same anger flaring in his eyes, like a spreading wildfire.

"I'm not standing for this," my squadron leader said, shaking his head. "No pilot should ever be forced to fly against his better judgment. It's dangerous and it jeopardizes everything we stand for. It's bad for everyone. It's bad for our future. This isn't the first time this kind of thing has happened. I've heard too many reports from the other guys, and now you're telling me this. I can't sit back and just watch this happen. I can't live with myself if something happens and I didn't speak up."

"But what the hell are we supposed to do?" I said, nearly shouting. "People like him know they hold all the power. They know we are at their mercy. They know they can treat us like cockroaches on a road, and there's not a single fucking thing we can do about it."

"Calm down. We're going to figure this out," my squadron leader said "We need to be logical and calculated. I'm going to write a letter to Saddam and explain the situation and ask that he take a stand against this behavior."

I sucked in a breath, suppressing the flames, harnessing the anger like I had a hundred times before. My squadron leader was right. That was the only thing we could do. I could only hope that it would work.

And at first, it seemed that it did. My squadron leader sent a letter explaining the situation and asking that an official statement be made to prevent this from happening again, and Saddam answered. A statement was released instructing all passengers on the VIP passenger list to adhere to safety protocols and respect all decisions made by the pilot concerning the flight.

We could only hope that it would prove to be effective.

And just a month later, it was put to the test.

I received instructions to prepare an aircraft to fly to Saudi

Arabia for none other than Sabawi. Immediate resentment rose in me at the mention of Sabawi's name.

"Sabawi? Are you kidding me?" I couldn't hide my feelings in front of my fellow pilots. "This guy is fucking crazy. Crazy! Do you remember what he did to me last time? The man made me fly in a FUCKING sandstorm!"

My friend nodded and put a hand on my shoulder and shook it gently.

"I know. I know," my friend said. "Just do what you know to do. Go be a pilot. It will be okay."

I nodded.

I inhaled, and as I exhaled I pushed the feelings deep, deep down. I had become a master of muzzling my voice, suppressing my anger, concealing my thoughts. I forced a look of neutrality onto my face.

I am a pilot. This is what I do.

And suddenly my mind went blank. I set about preparing the aircraft and making arrangements for the flight, a process that was more involved due to the fact that we'd be flying out of the country. I submitted a flight permission request to Saudi Arabia and then set to doing my series of checks and rechecks before takeoff, trying to prepare myself to face Sabawi as I watched the entourage of black vehicles pull into the airfield.

The sight of Sabawi's face gave me a pit in my stomach. There was something about Sabawi that was dark, his face like a window into a wicked and murky place. Wherever Sabawi walked, it seemed to spread. He boarded the plane, along with his security team of seven men, and took his seat.

But, once again, I had a problem. The aircraft was ready, but

I still hadn't received confirmation that my request for permission to fly over Saudi Arabia had been granted. And the rules are clear: there should be no flight until all permissions have been granted. Flying into Saudi Arabia airspace without permission is a dangerous matter, and there is a distinct possibility of being shot down.

That permission better come fast, I thought as I sat waiting. I didn't want to think about standing there and once again telling Sabawi we would have to wait for takeoff. After a few minutes, I checked again to see if the permission had come through, but it still had not. Every minute seemed like an hour.

Sabawi's bodyguard appeared beside me.

"Mr. Sabawi would like me to ask you why we have not taken off yet," the bodyguard said.

Here we go.

"Please inform Mr. Sabawi that we are waiting for permission to fly into Saudi Arabia airspace," I said.

The bodyguard said nothing and disappeared. He was back within minutes.

"Mr. Sabawi wants to see you."

My heart leapt into my throat, and I turned to my copilot in a panic.

"Maybe you should go," I said to him, thinking that a buffer between me and Sabawi might prevent something terrible from happening.

"Hell no," my copilot said, a look of fear glazing his eyes. "I'm not going anywhere near that man."

I had no choice. I took off my seatbelt and stoically walked to where Sabawi sat, my heart pounding. I tried to look calm. Sabawi's eyes sparked with nasty recognition at the sight of my face. He remembered me from the sandstorm incident.

"What is this I hear about permissions? Why are we not taking off? What permission are you talking about?" Sabawi asked. His voice was patronizing.

"Sir, we need permission to fly over Saudi Arabia airspace, and they have not yet granted it, I explained. "We need to wait until we receive confirmation, and then we can be on our way immediately."

My polite tone was an airtight dam for the thoughts and feelings I needed to hide.

"Huh," Sabawi said. His puffy face broke out into a cruel grin. He looked at me from head to toe, like a wolf considering how to grind a worm most efficiently into the ground.

Silence hung in the air for a moment. I looked at Sabawi, and Sabawi looked at me.

And then Sabawi's voice broke out into a shout: "GO!!!!!!! FLY THE PLANE! Get back in your seat and turn on your engine and fly this plane. Or maybe you can't fly. Is that it?" Then he sneered.

I tried not to blink, not to wince at Sabawi's bellowing voice. I didn't want to give him the satisfaction.

"What the fuck are these permissions you speak of? Just get in your seat AND FLY THE PLANE! FUUUUCKKK!" Sabawi screamed.

I felt Sabawi's screams throughout my entire body. Sabawi's eyes taunted me, daring me to give him one reason to channel his rage into action rather than just words. I could see the fact that Sabawi wanted to kill me. It was etched into every line of his terrible face.

Not here, not today.

I returned to my seat and fastened my seat belt, my hands shaking. Again, I was powerless. Again, I was being forced to jeopardize the safety of my aircraft and the lives of everyone aboard because of the insanity of a moronic man. But I didn't have the luxury of anger, of shaking hands, or rapid heart rate. I had to control myself. With a single breath, I took hold of every ounce of rage in my mind and body, and I forced it into submission.

Okay then. Let's do this.

Again, my mind went blank. I was no longer Mohammed with anger and emotion. I was a pilot. I was one with my craft. My mind, my hands, my eyes, and my ears were now part of the plane.

Down the runway we went, fast and smooth. And then we were airborne.

My heart rate increased with every minute as we flew closer and closer to the border of Saudi Arabia. Soon we approached the Compulsory Reporting Point, or CRP, which is a geographical point for which an aircraft must report its location. This point is designated by regulations on aeronautical charts by solid triangles or filed in a flight plan as fixes selected to define direct routes. They can be approved or deleted only by rule-making action.

I picked up the radio and attempted to make contact, hoping that by some miracle, we'd be granted permission. We were only ten minutes away from the border.

"You may continue as you are for now, but you still have not received permission to fly over Saudi airspace," the voice over the radio said, delivering the words I did not want to hear.

I had three choices now. I could go into a holding pattern and wait, I could turn the plane to Baghdad, or I could continue without permission and risk getting shot down.

I chose the first option and informed Sabawi that we would have to wait until we received permission to continue. Sabawi's expression was unreadable.

And then the wait began.

Ten minutes passed. No permission.

Twenty minutes passed. No permission.

I couldn't see Sabawi's face from my seat, but it was as if I could feel him, feel his anger permeating the entire plane.

Thirty minutes passed. Still no permission.

With every minute we stayed in a holding pattern, we were burning fuel. I had carefully planned the route and fuel amount, ensuring we had not only enough to get to our destination but also for two diversion routes in the case of an emergency.

Forty minutes passed. No permission.

Now there was only enough fuel for one diversion. The options were dwindling.

I couldn't stop the anger from pulsing through me as I sat waiting. I had been forced into yet another impossible scenario, forced to make choices he didn't want to make. I hated feeling powerless, at the mercy of a vicious, stupid man. The hatred entered my soul and ran through me until my hands began to shake with the force of suppressed rage. But I had to think clearly.

Ten more minutes. I'll give it ten more minutes, and then I'll tell him we have to return.

But even the thought of standing in front of those cold, evil eyes sent dread through my body.

Ten minutes. I watched the clock.

One minute, two minutes, three minutes, four minutes.

Suddenly a voice on the other end uttered the words I had been waiting to hear.

"Permission granted."

Relief flooded through me. I had been spared the wrath of Sabawi. But even the relief couldn't extinguish the venom in me from being nothing more than a puppet—something to be controlled and manipulated. I didn't want to be forced to play a game with life and death or danger and safety against my will.

The landing was smooth, and Sabawi exited without a word. I gritted my teeth and clenched my fist as if the tightened jaws and constricted fingers would help me contain the mounting hostility I felt inside.

Once Sabawi had left for his meetings, I completed the list of tasks to prepare the plane for another departure, which was scheduled for 7:00 p.m., and then I refreshed myself in the reception area, hoping a good meal and drink would calm me.

At 6:00 p.m., I made the final preparations. I turned on the equipment and began running the air conditioner to cool the plane down. At 7:00 p.m. sharp, we were ready to go. I scanned the road for the sight of Sabawi's black cars pulling into the airfield. But there was nothing.

Probably just a delay.

But then an hour passed. Another hour, still nothing.

We were now in danger of the plane overheating. I couldn't keep sitting there waiting. I turned off the equipment and allowed it to cool down for a while, but my heart raced as I did so. Sabawi could return at any minute, and if I didn't have his plane ready, I might have the shiny barrel of a gun pressed against my temples.

As soon as possible, I turned everything on again. But still no Sabawi. Another hour passed and I shut everything down to cool it again and then restarted it.

But no Sabawi.

I continued the cycle as the sky turned inky black.

On and then off.

On and then off.

On and then off.

My eyes felt gritty from the lack of sleep and my body grew weary. Midnight, 1:00 a.m., 2:00 a.m., 3:00 a.m., 4:00 a.m. I drank one cup of coffee and then another and another, but it did nothing to offset the exhaustion. With every passing hour, I looked to the road, expecting to see Sabawi's vehicles but nothing came.

And then the sun rose like the fury within me.

I am nothing more than a servant. A puppet, a bug to contain or crush.

I had been forced to fly into a sandstorm, to fly without permissions in a foreign airspace, and to stay awake through the night like a fool, starting and restarting a plane.

Then 6:00 a.m., and then 7:00 a.m. I turned everything on and then turned it off again.

At 8:00 a.m., a group of black vehicles approached. It was Sabawi, who had been scheduled to leave at 7:00 p.m. the previous night. I could feel my rage trying to find some way to escape, pressing against my ribs and lungs, making my throat feel tight.

Sabawi strode confidently out of the car with a smug look on his face and walked to where I stood, feeling like an idiot, eyes puffy from a sleepless night.

"Am I late?" Sabawi asked with an evil grin.

He was taunting me, daring me to say yes, to give him a reason to indulge his appetite for violence.

"No, sir," I replied.

"SHUT THE FUCK UP!" Sabawi screamed, viciously. "IF YOU SAY YES, I'LL KILL YOU."

Sabawi paused for a moment, his eyes twisted and deranged, searching my face. He wanted to do it. He wanted to kill me.

"Am I late?" Sabawi asked again.

"No, sir," I said, hating the lie as it came out of my mouth, hating my respectful tone, like a submissive dog.

Sabawi boarded the plane without another word.

I forced breath into my lungs, started the plane, and then took ff.

Once I reached cruising altitude, a deep wave of fatigue washed over me. I was tired. Tired from the night of missed sleep. Tired of being forced into terrible situations against my will. Tired of feeling powerless. Tired of being at the mercy of stupid, horrible men.

"You want a cup of coffee?" my copilot asked.

I shook my head wearily.

"I've already had a gallon of coffee. It's not going to change anything," I said.

After landing, I searched for my squad commander. When I found him, I told him everything.

"I'm reaching my point of limitation," I said. "I don't think I can keep doing this. This shouldn't be part of my job description. This shouldn't be my duty."

My squad commander sighed, his face looking almost as weary as mine.

"I wish I could do something. I wish I could find a way to fix this. But I already sent a letter, and it didn't do any good. This is Sabawi we're talking about. He's crazy. He'll fucking kill us if we cross him," my squad commander explained.

I nodded. I knew my squad commander was right. There wasn't anything we could do.

Part of me wanted to give up, to stop, to quit, to take back control. But where would that leave me? Where would I go? I had been given the opportunity of a lifetime. I was on the VIP squad. I was living every pilot's dream. The money was incredible, the gifts were generous, the prestige felt good.

So I did what I always did. I inhaled the anger, the hatred, the feelings of being powerless and swallowed them whole. Shoved them down where no one would see them.

I couldn't quit.

I had to keep going.

CHAPTER FIVE_

There are certain days in life that will forever become part of you. Days that imprint upon the mind like wet cement and only solidify with time. One of those days took place for me in the summer of 1987. I wish I could pinpoint the exact day, but time has rendered that detail fuzzy in my recollection. But I do remember with perfect clarity, however, the scorching summer sun and how it beat relentlessly down as I attended to my regular duties. Sweat dripped down my temples, and my chest felt heavy under the weight of the suffocating heat.

One of my close friends approached, wearing a special smile—the type of smile that betrays the fact there is a favor to be asked or request to be made. Any good friend knows this smile well.

"What's up?" I asked.

"Not much, my friend, not much," my friend said. His

smile widened even more until his teeth flashed. The request would be forthcoming at any moment now.

"So uh, Mohammed," he began, "I need to ask you a little favor."

I knew it.

"Could I get you to take my place on a mission today? It's my day off, and I'd like to get an early start driving home to Fallujah," my friend said.

Fallujah is about an hour's drive from Baghdad, and I knew my friend was eager to see his family and rest after working a long shift of consecutive days.

"Consider it done." I smiled and patted my friend on the back.

My friend's face lit up. "Thank you so much. I will repay you; I promise. Anytime you need someone to take your place, ask me and I will do it."

I knew my friend meant what he said. We shared a close camaraderie between us, we had each other's back no matter what.

"What kind of mission is it?" I asked out of curiosity.

"It's a special mission of some kind. I haven't been given details yet. I just know it's somebody from P2," my friend said.

I nodded. Perhaps it would be a minister or high-ranking member of the army. I was accustomed to flying these types of missions and gave it little thought.

I prepared the aircraft for the flight, working my way through the list of preflight preparations and procedures. I still had not been informed as to who exactly I would be flying or where we would be going. I only knew I needed to have an aircraft ready for a special mission beside the P2 reception and that it would be a domestic flight. That meant there was no need to prepare for a long flight or request permission for flying into foreign airspace.

Customarily, the passenger usually arrived by car and was escorted by the wing commander through the reception area and to the plane. The aircraft was prepped and ready to go by noon, and I sat waiting and scanning the area for the arrival of my passenger. I blasted the air conditioner on my damp face, attempting to push away the exhaustion the persistent heat had created in my body. After an hour and a half, I heard the sound of an approaching helicopter. I had been expecting to see a line of vehicles approach the reception area. I craned my neck to try and get a look the helicopter. From my window, I captured a quick glance of it as it descended. It was from the palace. I sat up straight in my seat. This was not an ordinary P2 mission.

The helicopter landed beside my plane, and I felt suddenly anxious. I had been prepared for a normal P2 mission, prepared to fly a minister or army official, but this was all different. This had to be someone from the palace. We hadn't been informed to prepare for a VIP of this caliber, and no one was ready for it. No wing commander ready to greet and escort the passenger to the plane, no big reception waiting.

The helicopter landed on the right side of the aircraft. Again, I tried to get a look at who was inside, but the bright sunlight reflected off the windows. I could only make out shapes and silhouettes, no particular people or recognizable faces.

"Can you see anything?" I asked my copilot, whose

window view was unobstructed.

"Hmmm, I don't know," my copilot said, straining to see. "Wait! Wait! Yeah, I see it now. It's Saddam!" He looked at me with wide eyes.

I jumped. All heat-induced malaise drained immediately from my body, and my heart began to pound.

"Really? Are you sure?" I asked.

"It's definitely Saddam," my copilot said as his spine straightened and his body stiffened in readiness. Mine did the same.

Questions filled my mind: *What was this mission? Why had he arrived without announcement? Why were we departing from P2 reception instead of P1 where the royal family typically departs from?*

I kept straining to see out of my copilot's window, to get a glance of King Saddam Hussein himself.

And suddenly, he was there.

Saddam was dressed in a suit, something I had never seen him wear. I had only ever seen Saddam dressed in a military uniform. Two bodyguards walked on either side of him as he approached the plane.

I sat stiffly, every sense in my body on high alert as Saddam climbed the stairs. My heart beat erratically, and my palms began to sweat.

Stay calm. Stay calm.

I felt hyper aware of every millimeter I moved, every twitch of my arms and legs. One wrong move, one wrongly perceived behavior and the bodyguards would waste no time in ending my life on the spot. I felt small, my entire being at the mercy of a madman.

Suddenly Saddam was standing there. The dictator himself—living and breathing before me, staring at me with those brown eyes.

"Hello! How are you today?" Saddam's voice boomed into the quiet plane.

"I am good, sir, very good. And how are you?" I forced my voice.

"Do you know where you're going today?" Saddam asked.

"No, sir, I do not." My voice sounded small and hollow.

"Fly to Habbaniya Air Force Base," Saddam said. "Okay?"

"Yes, sir." I nodded.

"Then let's go."

It was a command. Saddam made his way to his seat, and I looked at my copilot whose eyes reflected my own anxiety. The flight engineer closed the hatch, and my hands moved mechanically as I prepared for takeoff.

In no time we were taxiing down the runway. And then smooth as silk, we took flight. The distance from Baghdad to Habbaniya is only about eighty kilometers. It was going to be a quick flight. I wasted no time in establishing contact and requesting permission to land.

"This is Bravo 1-8, requesting permission to land," I radioed into the tower.

"Bravo 1-8 permission granted; you are clear to land," a voice boomed back over the radio almost immediately.

I guided the plane down for landing, taking extra care to ensure that it was steady and gentle. It was perfect.

Once on the ground, I looked out the window, expecting to see the normal hustle and bustle of the airbase.

But there was nothing.

Not a sound, not a hint of movement, not a single person in sight. The silence was eerie, and I felt my breath catch in my lungs. This was no ordinary transportation mission. It was just me, my copilot, and the flight engineer alone with one of the most powerful and vicious dictators in the world. The entire area had obviously been evacuated in preparation for Saddam's arrival. My skin felt clammy and uncomfortable. I looked at my copilot, who was staring out of the window. We didn't say a word. A look passed between us that didn't need verbal explanation. This was not a normal mission. Great lengths had been taken to ensure total secrecy. Minimal bodyguards, total evacuation in all directions.

I felt a slow and terrifying sensation spread through me as I realized I was about to see something I should not be seeing, something that was very dangerous, something that very powerful people had taken painstaking measures to ensure was kept a secret. And that's when I realized that if I wanted to make it through the day alive, I had better become invisible. No probing eyes, no curious glances, no look that would even suggest that I understood what was going on around me. I would have to become inhuman, robotic. As if my eyes could see nothing, and my ears could hear nothing.

I stiffened and nodded at my copilot. He understood.

As I exited the runway, I noticed another aircraft like ours parked in the distance.

"Go park next to that aircraft," Saddam said, his low voice suddenly behind me.

I see nothing, and I hear nothing.

"Yes, sir," I said and began to taxi in that direction.

I parked to the right of the plane and tried to steal a better look for some indication of who was inside but couldn't make anything out. Our flight engineer opened the door and pulled out the stairs in preparation for Saddam to exit the plane.

I immediately cut off the engines, even the sound of idling felt too conspicuous, as if it would draw more attention to my presence. Invisible. I just wanted to be invisible.

Saddam exited the aircraft, and just as he did, two figures appeared from the other aircraft directly adjacent to us. At first, I couldn't see the faces well but as they drew closer to Saddam, I suddenly recognized who it was. I knew that face. I had seen it on the front of magazines and on the news more times than I could count.

"Do you see who that is?" I hissed to my copilot. His face was white, and his eyes were wide with surprise.

"That's Yitzhak Rabin, the Israeli prime minister."

We held each other's gaze for a moment, our minds racing.

Why would Saddam have a private meeting with the man who was supposedly his enemy?

The tensions between our two nations are as old as time. I knew as well as every citizen in our nation that Iraq was not on good terms with the Israeli people. It was no secret they regarded Saddam as a danger and threat to their national security. And yet there Rabin was, walking out into the open, hardly accompanied by security to meet Saddam.

I couldn't take my eyes away.

Rabin walked toward Saddam, and Saddam walked toward Rabin. They met in the middle, between the two aircrafts.

Immediately they pulled in for a quick embrace as they shook hands. There was something familiar in the way they moved, almost as if they were old friends. I couldn't believe my eyes.

I couldn't hear their voices, but I could see their mouths moving as they launched into immediate conversation. Rabin broke out into a wide grin and said something to Saddam. Saddam threw his head back and laughed heartily. The intimacy of their exchange shocked me. I knew of the relationship between Iraq and Israel. I always imagined that a meeting of our two leaders would be stoic, tense, full of anger and hatred. And yet here I sat, watching their private exchange, watching as the two men talked, laughed, and joked. It was difficult to comprehend.

After chatting casually for a few minutes between the two aircraft, Rabin and Saddam made their way to Rabin's plane and boarded it together. I sat, my mind racing with questions: *What were they talking about? Why were they meeting privately like this? What if someone found out about this meeting and blamed me for leaking the information?*

One hour passed. Then two. I began to wonder how long they intended to talk. My copilot and I tried to keep a conversation going to fill the silence, but there was no relief for the tension and anxiety that coiled itself around us. After two and a half hours, Saddam and Rabin emerged from Rabin's aircraft and began to walk. They never broke conversation. They walked out in front of both planes and then toward our aircraft. Once they neared the plane, they turned and walked back out again. Back and forth, back and forth they paced, never interrupting the stream of conversation between them.

They were engrossed. They paused for a few minutes in between the planes as Rabin finished saying something, and Saddam listened thoughtfully. Then Rabin threw his head back and laughed heartily, and Saddam joined in.

I turned on the APU, or Auxiliary Power Unit, to create a bit of background noise without drawing too much attention to where my copilot and I sat waiting and watching.

I felt a knot building in my stomach. There were only three of us who were witnesses to this meeting: me, my copilot, and the flight engineer. Three people who could easily be made to disappear. If the details of this meeting were to go public, it would be a disaster. I knew that all too well. I had become a loose end. We were all loose ends.

Were we the disposable personnel selected for this mission? Here for a one-time use and then to be thrown away to keep things easy and clean? The thought was haunting, maddening.

I looked around again at the deserted airfield. Careful planning had been invested into this meeting to ensure there were absolutely no witnesses. Except for me, my copilot, and the flight engineer.

Part of me wanted the entire mission to be over. To be far from Saddam and his bodyguards. But another part of me dreaded the end of the mission because I feared that it would also be the end of my life. I meant nothing to Saddam. I was just the young man who flew the plane. I was a life that in Saddam's eyes could easily be sacrificed. I was totally and utterly disposable.

And that was a crushing truth to accept. That you, with all your hopes, dreams, and desires, are nothing more than a cog in a wheel and a means to an end in a much bigger scheme. You with your wife and young children at home, with the father who loves you, with the big plans for your life that could be thrown away in an instant for the sheer sake of convenience.

I don't want to die for this.

I watched the two men again as they paused their pacing not far from the plane. Rabin extended his hand to Saddam, and Saddam shook it with a smile. Then the two embraced. Arms around one another for several moments.

I couldn't believe what I was seeing. Where was the hate? Where were the tensions? Where was all the mistrust and anger that was supposed to be between our two nations? I didn't know what to make of the friendly exchange and the familiarity of their manner with one another.

Saddam waved goodbye to Rabin and then turned and walked back toward our aircraft. He boarded with a smile on his face.

"Wait and let Rabin take off first," Saddam said. "Then we will go."

"Yes, sir," I said and immediately set to work.

Mohammed attempted to contact the tower in preparation for takeoff, but there was no answer. Every single person had been removed from the area. This was all entirely up to me.

Once Rabin's aircraft had taken off, we began to taxi down the runway. No communication, no sound but the power of the engine as we took flight. I felt a small sense of satisfaction at the smoothness of my takeoff. A feeling of heaviness hung in the air during the short flight back to

Baghdad. None of us were sure what would happen next once we landed.

The landing was beautiful. I only hoped that it would not be my last.

I landed near P1 reception and immediately six black vehicles appeared to take Saddam. My chest felt tight. The flight engineer opened the door. I could hear Saddam's footsteps as he neared the cockpit, but I willed myself to keep staring ahead.

Then I felt a hand on my shoulder. I tried not to bristle or jump, to breathe evenly. But my pulse skyrocketed rebelliously. Saddam stood hovering, one hand on my shoulder, one on the shoulder of my copilot, who sat woodenly. His eyes reflected the fear I felt.

"Guys, did you see anything today?" Saddam asked casually, as if he were inquiring about our lunch order. But even the gentleness in his tone was laced with something evil, threatening.

"No, sir. We didn't see anything," I said, hoping with everything in me that I sounded convincing.

"Good. Very good," Saddam said.

Saddam lifted his hand and then brought it back down softly on my shoulder like a fatherly pat. I fisted my palms so that their shaking would not be visible. I didn't want Saddam to see my fear.

And then Saddam was gone. He climbed into one of the waiting vehicles, and they drove away in confusing patterns until I couldn't tell which one Saddam was in.

Once Saddam was out of eyeshot, I turned to my copilot.

"This is a bad situation we're in. Really bad."

My hands were still shaking.

"Look at me," I said fiercely, and my copilot turned and faced me. "You cannot say a word about this, do you hear me? We can never speak about what we saw today. Please, please, please, I beg of you. Do not say a word. If this gets out, they will immediately be able to track the leak back to us, and we'll have our lives to pay for it."

"I won't, I won't," my copilot said. "I'm scared too. I'm not going to breathe a word about this."

"You have to understand that this isn't a joke," I said, my voice solemn. "This is serious, do you understand that? If word gets out about this meeting, we will be blamed. Not only will it be a disaster in the press, but they will lose all trust in us, and all of us will be killed."

The faces of my daughters flashed through my mind. I suddenly ached to see them. I hated the idea of entrusting my future to someone else's ability to hold their tongue, but I had no choice.

Fear built up in my copilot's eyes as I spoke. He raked his palms across his knees rhythmically and rocked back and forth.

"Oh shit, oh shit. Mohammed, this is not good. This is not good at all. They are going to kill us! They will do it, those fucking bastards, and there's nothing we can do about it," my pilot said. He was starting to become hysterical. "I hate them. I hate them all. There's nothing we can do to save ourselves. Not a damn thing."

I understood the look of helpless fear in his eyes and how it induced a fiery rage inside because I felt it myself—the fear and anger.

"Calm down," I said. "We have to be rational about this. You can't let this anger take hold of you, or you're going to do something you're going to regret. Swallow the anger, and whatever you do, don't breathe a word of this to anyone."

I spoke the same grim warning to the flight engineer as well, who swore his silence. We all nodded at one another as we prepared to leave. This day could never, ever be spoken of again. There was nothing more I could do but trust that they would keep their word. We were all trusting each other with our lives.

I walked away with a pit in my stomach.

Sleep did not come easy that night. I could still feel Saddam's hand on my shoulder and hear the dictator's whisper in my ear.

"Did you see anything today?"

"Did you see anything today?"

"Did you see anything today?"

The question played in my head like a broken tape recorder. I jumped at every noise, every sound, afraid that someone was coming for me.

The next day I awoke and dressed and headed to work, trying to carry on as normally as possible. I nodded at my copilot knowingly when I saw him, and he nodded back.

"Hey, by the way, what was your mission yesterday?" our squadron leader asked.

My copilot's face froze for a split second as he caught eyes with me. The question was not uncommon. we often discussed our missions with each other. But it was the first time we had been asked about it.

"Someone from the delegation. I can't remember the name now," I said lazily.

My squadron leader nodded and moved on, unimpressed. I gave my copilot a hard stare.

"That's how we do it," I whispered. "That's how we do it."

My copilot nodded.

That same day a man approached me and handed me an envelope. "For you and your friend," he said.

A few days later, I returned home to my wife and children, but it only made the fear and anxiety worse. I entered my house carefully, checking every room for signs of something being amiss. My senses always remained on high alert. Each time the doorbell rang my hands would shake and my heart would pound. Every phone call, every lingering glance from a stranger in the street, every late-night noise caused me to panic.

Only three people. Only three people know about the top-secret meeting between Saddam and Rabin. And I am one of them. I am nothing more than a loose end, a liability. Only three people.

That weekend, I saw my friend, the one who had asked me to take his place for the mission.

"How did the flight go?" my friend asked. "Who did you end up flying?"

"Just someone from the delegation," I said, trying to sound relaxed. "How was your time with your family?"

"It started off terribly," my friend said. "I was hoping to get there early, but they shut down all the roads west of Baghdad for hours. They wouldn't even let anyone drive. It was ridiculous. I was sitting in the car for hours."

Understanding dawned in my mind.

That's why I didn't see anyone on the road or in the airfield.

They had shut down all the roads for miles just for that meeting between Saddam and Rabin to ensure total safety and privacy. I shuffled my feet and tried to play it off coolly.

"Very strange," I said with a feigned puzzled expression.

The fear and anxiety didn't subside that week or in the weeks that followed. I lived with constant paranoia.

Three months later, my friend approached me. "So, I've been hearing reports circulating," he said. "Remember that day you took my place for flying? People are saying that Saddam had a secret meeting with Israeli Prime Minister Rabin that day."

My stomach twisted, and my throat felt tight.

"Really?" I manufactured a look of shock. "That's crazy! I haven't heard anything about it."

My friend continued to prattle on. But my mind was frozen, and my blood ran cold.

How did this get out? Who was talking?

Dread spread through my body. Just when I had begun to breathe a little easier, just when I thought I was in the clear, new reports were circulating that would place me under immediate suspicion.

And so, fear became my constant companion. Every day that I laid my head down on my pillow, still alive and breathing, I thought: *It wasn't today. Thank God it wasn't today. Tomorrow is a new day. It will probably be tomorrow.*

CHAPTER SIX_

Sometimes I think I was meant to be a bird. My body, mind, and soul have craved the sky since I was a child, and I feel more at home there than anywhere on solid ground. Over the course of the seven years that I served as a pilot on the VIP squad, I logged in more than 3,500 flight hours, which was far beyond average.

Out of all those thousands of hours, there are flights that stick out in my memory because they were dangerous, secretive, or risky. And then there are those that stick out for *other reasons*.

In the summer of the late 1980s, I received orders to fly the Minister of Communication, Mohammed Hamza Zubeidi, from Baghdad to Delhi, India. It was a long flight with several stops along the way, but we made it safely to Delhi and stayed for a few days so that the Minister could conduct his business. On the fourth day, I received my orders to ready the aircraft for our return flight. I arrived early, just as I always did, so that I could take my time with the preflight procedures and have time to sip a cup of coffee.

As I went about my usual routine, I heard a low engine sound in the distance and noticed a pickup truck rumbling toward the plane. When it stopped, a man hopped out and approached the aircraft with a huge smile.

"Hello!" the man called. "I am coming from the Iraqi Embassy with a delivery for the Minister."

He immediately walked around to the back of the truck and opened it up. I strained my eyes as I tried to process what appeared to be stacks of cages. Animal cages. A screeching sound erupted as the man grabbed two of the crates and began to load them into the plane.

And then I got a better look at what was inside.

A dirty looking monkey in one and a parrot in the other.

I stood speechless for a few moments. Never had I had cargo like this in one of my planes.

"It's for the Minister!" said the man from the embassy enthusiastically, as if that explained the fact that about a dozen cages filled with monkeys and parrots were being loaded onto my plane.

"Where do you want me to put them?" the man asked.

I blinked a couple of times and then sprang into action and bounded onto the plane ahead of him. This was no ordinary plane he was loading animals onto. It was a beautiful VIP aircraft, complete with every kind of luxurious finish imaginable. The seats were made of elephant leather. Shiny gold and crystal finishes sparkled throughout the entire interior. I couldn't have monkeys and parrots running around.

"Where the hell are we supposed to put these?" I asked the flight engineer, whose expression of shock and alarm mirrored mine.

"All I know is that if we set these cages on the seats, they will destroy the upholstery," the fight engineer said.

We were going to have to get creative.

We searched and found sheets of plastic and draped them over the seats to create a seating area for our uncommon passengers and then started loading the cages. By the time all the animals had boarded, there were only two seats left empty —one for the Minister and one for his secretary. The entire room was filled with screeching and squawking and a freakshow of movement. I couldn't hear myself think.

I then resumed my preflight check only to hear yet another low engine in the distance and to see another pickup truck rumbling toward the plane.

Again, another man hopped out with a big smile on his face.

"I am coming from the Iraqi Embassy with a delivery for the Minister," the man said.

Of course, you are.

Out of the back of the truck came more monkeys and more parrots.

It was back to the drawing board on our seating arrangement. We repositioned this cage here and shoved this cage there and finally fit them all inside. We tied down the cages with rope to keep them in position. The room was packed, and it was loud. Screeches, squawks, and screams echoed throughout the room. But that wasn't even the worst part.

The smell.

I can still remember that unmistakable odor of wild animal feces, farts, and unwashed behinds. It was positively suffocating. I was ready to escape, and we hadn't even taken off yet.

"Check the locks on every cage," I said to the flight engineer. "We can't afford to have a monkey running into the cockpit."

The flight engineer checked over each cage while I finished the preflight procedures.

And then I sat, waiting for the Minister to arrive, listening to the symphony of screeches behind me.

This is going to be a long flight.

And then I noticed something.

Every time the monkeys would make a noise, the parrots would attempt to repeat it.

Over and over and over again.

Screeching monkey. Parrot imitation of screeching monkey.

Screeching monkey. Parrot imitation of screeching monkey.

Screeching monkey. Parrot imitation of screeching monkey.

It was a jungle.

"How the hell is control going to hear a single thing we say over the radio with this zoo going on?" my copilot asked.

"We'll just have to shut the door and hope for the best," I said, shaking my head.

What has my life come to?

Finally, the Minister boarded, and we were off. It was a smooth takeoff, and we reached cruising altitude without a hitch.

But the noise never stopped.

Screeching monkey. Parrot imitation of screeching monkey.
Screeching monkey. Parrot imitation of screeching monkey.
Screeching monkey. Parrot imitation of screeching monkey.

It played on an endless loop.

And even with the cockpit door closed, the stench seeped through the cracks and infused every breath with a smell so bad we could almost taste it.

Each hour passed agonizingly slow.

After a while, nature began to call from the direction of my bladder, and I turned things over to my copilot so I could excuse myself to the bathroom. To get there, I had to walk right through the main cabin. I braced myself as I opened the cockpit door.

A more potent variant of the smell smacked me in the face. I scanned the room, and to my horror, there were food pellets and seeds scattered around the entire room, adding to the stench.

The Minister was on his feet, peering into one of the monkey cages.

"Hello, sir, how are you?" I asked.

The Minister tossed me a quick smile and then continued cooing and chatting with the monkey. I shifted my feet, my bladder uncomfortably full. The Minister was blocking my path to the bathroom, but I didn't want to appear impolite by asking the Minister to move.

"This is my hobby, you know," the Minister said suddenly, not breaking his gaze from the monkey's cage. "I love them. I just love them."

"That's very nice, sir," I said respectfully.

The Minister stood tall and looked at me. His eyes were hazy from alcohol, and his voice was thick and syrupy.

"I love them like family," the Minister said, thick with emotion. "I really do. I love them like family."

I looked from the Minister to the array of dirty, squawking animals and then back.

What the fuck? Was he serious?

I searched the Minister's eyes but found no hint of irony there. Nothing but pure love and affection.

The Minister placed his hand mindlessly on one of the cages and continued, "They mean so much to me. I can't explain it. They really are like my family."

I just stood there, unsure what to say, desperately wanting to pee. I looked toward the Minister's bare hand resting on the cage to try and avoid eye contact. Just as I did, the monkey inside reached out and grabbed the Minister's hand.

"MOTHERFUCKER!" the Minister shouted as he jerked his hand away from the cage.

His face was livid with anger.

What did you expect?

The Minister's other fist slammed into the cage.

"MOTHERFUCKER!" he said again.

For a brief moment, the monkey paused, staring straight at the Minister's face. Then with perfect precision, the monkey grabbed a chunk of food from his mouth and threw it squarely onto the Minister's arm.

Laughter bubbled up inside of me. The sight of the Minister having a lover's quarrel and food fight with a monkey was more than I could handle. I couldn't stop myself. Peals of laughter rang out so intense that my belly shook and tears streamed down my face.

The Minister looked down at the saliva-ridden wad of food on his arm, and his face turned an even darker shade of red.

"YOU MOTHERFUCKER! YOU MOTHERFUCKER!" the Minister shouted.

He slammed his fist into the cage again and then grabbed a hold of it and started to shake it.

"MOTHERFUCKER!" he screamed again.

The monkey wasted no time in retaliating. Another fistful of food flew through the air and onto the Minister's chest.

Another fist onto the cage.

Another fistful of food flew through the air.

My belly hurt from laughing, and my bladder felt as if it would explode.

"Please, sir, please," I said, "you have to calm down."

I pulled the Minister away from the cage and guided him to his seat. He swayed a bit, his face still red and angry.

Once seated, the Minister seemed to calm down.

I wasted no time in running to the bathroom to relieve myself. As soon as I finished, I made my way back to the cockpit and relayed the story to my copilot, who bent over in peals of laughter.

"Our job is so strange sometimes," my copilot said.

He was right. In addition to flying in the middle of a sandstorm, landing in Somalia in the middle of a coup, and transporting Saddam to a top-secret meeting, I could now add flying monkeys, parrots, and a minister with a love-hate relationship with his pets to the list.

When it came time to radio in for landing, the control tower could barely make out my words over the squeaking and squawking. My copilot and I could only laugh at our situation.

Once on the ground in Baghdad, the crew approached to help with the deboarding process.

"What the hell is in there?" asked one of the flight engineers as the zoo animal noises echoed from within the plane.

"Ah, just some monkeys and a handful of parrots," I said casually. "The Minister says he loves them like family."

I proceeded to relay the entire story of loading the animals into the plane and the fight between the monkey and the Minister.

The flight engineer laughed uncontrollably just as I had.

It took hours to professionally clean that plane and two more days after that for the interior to properly air out and dry. Even still, it seemed as if the smell lingered.

After that day, if there was ever a suspicious smell inside of an aircraft, we called it "monkey plane."

None of us could ever forget that smell.

Days like that made life colorful and interesting. I always had a feeling that anything could happen. Sometimes that was a good thing. To know that I might get to meet someone famous and noteworthy or receive a generous bonus if performed above and beyond in my service. Sometimes it was not a good thing. To know that I could be blamed for a security leak if the details about Saddam's secret meeting with the Israeli Prime Minister ever got out or that my life could be on the line if I dared to make the wrong person angry.

There was always a war within me. Between loving my job and hating it. I loved flying, I loved getting to travel the world and meet interesting people, I loved the money that I was earning for my family. But I hated the feeling of being out of control and being at the mercy of stupid, powerful men. Even still, the benefits of the job still outweighed the negative aspects. I was able to build a beautiful house for my family and return from my travels with gifts that made my wife smile and my children squeal. I loved that.

Once, I even took my wife on a private ride in one of my favorite aircrafts at Firnas Aero Club. I relished the look of pride on her face as she buckled in beside me. It was a big pleasure for me to see my woman next to me, smiling and proud. It made me want to show off a little, to flex the proverbial muscles and show my girl what I was capable of.

As my wife buckled into the seat behind me, I mentally began to plan the maneuvers I would do, the ways I would show her things she had never seen.

"All set back there?" I called as we prepared for takeoff.

"I'm all set!" my wife said brightly.

Takeoff was perfect. We climbed in the air like a bird taking flight. Then it was time to show off a little.

"Are you ready for some fun?" I asked loudly over the sound of the engine.

"I'm ready!" my wife said with a giggle.

Then I went for it. I pulled out all the stops. I did loops, spins, rolls, and lines.

The rush of pulling off a risky maneuver never got old for me. I craved the powerful feeling of g-force pinning me back in my seat and the way my pulse pounded with adrenaline.

The backseat was quiet. Not a single sound from my wife's mouth.

I've left her speechless. She must be really happy.

I did a few more maneuvers to finish off the trip and then touched back down on the ground with satisfaction. Still not a sound from my wife.

I hopped from my seat and opened the door to help my wife unbuckle from the harnesses, eagerly awaiting her big smile. But there was no smile on her face. Her lips were drawn, and her head pressed into the seat behind her awkwardly as if it hadn't moved since being pinned back by the g-force power. Her face was as white as winter snow.

"Are you okay?" I asked, surprised.

She inhaled weakly and paused for just a moment as she met my eyes.

"Fuck you," she finally whispered. "Fuck you."

"What happened to you?" I asked, thoroughly confused.

"Fuck you," she said again, shaking her head. "What the hell did you put me through? I almost died up there."

"Why didn't you tell me?" I asked. "Why didn't you let me know you weren't comfortable?"

She glared at me.

"Because I was pinned down, Mohammed, that's why. I

couldn't lift my head or even reach to communicate with you," she said.

I couldn't help but laugh. But, of course, it only made my wife angrier. She was nauseous and sick to her stomach for hours. My flexing and showing off for my girl did not have the effect I was hoping for. One person's pleasure is another person's pain.

But still I loved the fact I had that kind of position and prestige to be able to fly my woman into the sky and provide well for her and my children. It made me show up another day and another day and another day, even when things were hard, even when fear gnawed at my belly.

Another day that sticks out in my memory as possibly even more strange and unexpected than flying cages full of monkeys and parrots is the time I walked in on the great and brutal dictator Saddam Hussein naked.

The year was 1987, and I was given an order to fly Saddam from Baghdad to a secret location in the north of Iraq. No one knew Saddam was there or what he was doing, and I didn't ask questions. I just followed orders and said no more than absolutely necessary.

"Yes, sir."

"No, sir."

"Very good, sir."

I clung to these few words like a lifeline. I didn't want to draw more attention to myself than necessary. Each time I was tasked with piloting a top-secret mission, I had yet another reason to watch my back, to fear the repercussions that I would face if any of the details of the flight ever became public knowledge. If any information was leaked, blame would be immediately placed upon my shoulders, and the punishment would be severe.

The flight commenced without a hitch, and we landed safely at the airbase in the north of Iraq. After landing, we opened the doors and extended the stairs from the aircraft to the ground.

We waited for Saddam to emerge from the VIP seating section, but he didn't come.

We waited a little bit longer.

Still no Saddam.

Gingerly, I stood up and walked back toward the VIP section to see what was going on. I didn't want to disturb Saddam, but it was strange that he hadn't yet emerged. The door of the VIP seating area was closed.

Shit.

No one ever shut the door to the VIP seating area. It always stayed open. Immediately, I remembered the door had a reputation for getting stuck once it was closed, making it so that no one could open it from the inside. I had spoken with the flight engineer about it, and he had attempted to fix it but to no avail. It hadn't seemed like a pressing problem at the time because no one ever used it. But now I was panicking.

Was Saddam locked in the room and unable to get out?

If so, he'd be irate, furious, murderously angry.

Saddam was already late for exiting the plane. The airbase commander and wing commander were all waiting. And Saddam was likely locked inside the room. I had to do something fast.

"Go open the door," I said to the wing commander.

"Fuck no!" the wing commander said. "Are you crazy? I'm not going to open that door!"

Inwardly, I groaned. It had to be me.

I took a deep breath and nodded toward my wing commander.

"Okay, I'm going in," I said.

My pulse quickened as I approached the door. I gave it a push. I felt resistance.

So I pushed harder.

I have to get to him.

Suddenly, the door gave in, and I tumbled into the room.

"Hey, hey, stop!" Saddam's voice rang out. Suddenly, we were eye to eye.

With horror, I took in the sight in front of me.

The naked, exposed form of the powerful dictator stooped over in nothing but a pair of underwear. My mind couldn't process what I was seeing.

It was obvious I had caught him in the middle of changing his uniform. My heart beat wildly. In my panic to make sure Saddam hadn't been locked into the room, I had made a huge mistake and committed a terrible breach of privacy.

Fear coursed through me.

For a terrible, agonizing moment, all I could do was stare into Saddam's shocked face as he stood before me bare-skinned and raw.

"I'm sorry, sir, I am so sorry." My words came tumbling out in a breathless rush. "I thought you were locked in the room.

This door doesn't work sometimes, you see, and I, well, I thought...I'm so sorry, sir."

My body tensed as I braced myself for what would come next.

Saddam looked at me for a moment

"Wait outside the door, and I'll be ready soon," Saddam said.

I didn't linger for even half a second. I disappeared from the room as fast as possible, my heart still beating wildly in my chest. I waited nervously just outside the door. My palms were sweaty, and I rehearsed my speech, my plea to explain my sudden intrusion.

After a few minutes, the handle clicked and Saddam emerged, wearing his traditional uniform.

"I'm so sorry, sir, I'm so sorry. When that door closes, it can't be opened from the inside, and I thought you were stuck. My apologies, sir," I said.

"I was behind the door, changing," Saddam said, staring straight into my eyes.

"I know, sir, and I'm so sorry, sir." I wanted to say more, but I didn't know what more I could say. I had intruded upon Saddam's privacy. I had burst into the room unannounced. I had seen him practically *naked*. I waited tensely for him to respond.

Saddam broke out into a generous smile.

"It's alright, it's alright, my boy," he said.

He gave me a nod. A nod of mercy, a nod that sent relief through my entire body. Saddam knew I had made a simple mistake with the best of intentions. He wasn't angry or upset; he was amused.

Saddam exited the plane, and I stood for a minute, slowing my breathing and steading my pulse. I had flown Saddam on many occasions and, yet again, he was friendly, polite, understanding, and at ease. It was hard to reconcile that the same brutal dictator who could kill, torture, and slaughter people in inhumane and unthinkable ways was the man smiling and patting me on the shoulder.

I received a large bonus after that flight. My loyalty strengthened again, just as they knew it would. More money for my wife and children, more money to build us a strong future.

Does Saddam have a nice side? Could he be a better man than we believed him to be?

My mind was still trying to connect the barbaric tyrant I watched and read about on television with the smiling man I had come face-to-face with.

Not long after, shocking news circulated through the entire country. Adnan Khairallah, Saddam's brother-in-law and cousin, had died in a helicopter crash. He had held several titles and was a member of the Iraqi Revolutionary Command Council and served as the Defense Minister of Iraq. The helicopter crash was officially labeled an accident, but no one believed that story, not even for a moment.

Saddam referred to him as one of the distinguished war heroes and a sparkling star in Iraq's sky when he announced the tragic death. His face looked sympathetic, full of honor and decorum. But there wasn't a doubt in my mind that Saddam had personally ordered Khairallah's death.

The circumstances surrounding his death, including his disputes with Saddam and rumors of a potential coup, led many of us to believe Khairallah was assassinated under orders from Saddam, and speculation circulated that his death was caused due to the detonation of four explosive charges of the helicopter he was in. There were rumors of a family rift and even talk of a coup. The people loved Khairallah, and he was powerful. Too powerful for Saddam, it seemed.

I sat back in my seat after reading the reports of Khairallah's death, my mind reeling.

This is the man that rode in the back of your plane. This is the man you serve. A man that would kill his own family members for his personal gain.

It was a disturbing thought, one that lodged itself into my mind and in the pit of my stomach. I was on the right side *for now*. I was in the inner circle. I was among the trusted few to be granted access to some of the most powerful people on earth.

But what would happen if I ever turned up on the wrong side?

CHAPTER SEVEN_

In late July of 1990, I received orders to fly Yasser Arafat to Cairo. In the months prior, sparks between the Iraqi government and Kuwait had ignited over the lucrative oil supply in Kuwait, and all of us feared a raging fire that would ensue if tensions continued to rise. As speculations of military involvement and escalation began to circulate, Yasser Arafat scheduled numerous meetings in an attempt to help calm the tension.

And I was his pilot.

After visiting Cairo for several days, Arafat was joined by another minister, and I flew them both to Kuwait for another round of meetings and talks. The flight went off without a hitch and all of us were transported to a grand reception in a beautiful building not far away. The Minister and Yasser Arafat immediately began their appointed meetings, and I walked around, admiring the impressive architecture and opulence of the building. I marveled at the magnificent door that opened into the large entryway and how it appeared to be one solid piece. It was a perk of the job—getting to see so many incredible and impressive places across the world.

After about four hours, Arafat appeared again, and we made our way back to the aircraft for the quick flight back to Baghdad. I could only hope these talks would result in peaceful resolution.

But nothing changed.

The deep lines on Arafat's face as he boarded the plane confirmed my worst fears. The situation was bad, and it was not getting any better.

"It's bad, very bad," Arafat said.

My chest felt heavy.

Arafat looked worn and exhausted.

"Don't come at 8:00 a.m. tomorrow," Arafat said when we landed. "I'm tired. I need to rest."

I nodded. It was already late, and we had kept a grueling schedule for days on end. As soon as I finished my post-flight procedures, I headed home and crashed into bed.

I awoke at about 7:00 a.m. the next morning on August 2. I showered, gathered my things and then began the forty-minute drive from my house back to the airbase.

Absentmindedly, I flipped on the radio, looking for background noise to help pass the time. Within seconds, I knew something was wrong. Reports were flying in about what had happened during the night, and my brain strained, trying to make sense of it all.

I jumped from my vehicle as soon as I arrived at the airbase and bounded inside.

"What the hell is going on?" I asked at the sight of the first familiar face.

"Not even ten minutes after you left the airbase last night, we invaded Kuwait," my friend told me. His face looked grim.

"No one knew about this," my friend said. "None of us had any idea he was going to do this."

I soon learned the whole story. At 2:00 a.m. Iraqi forces invaded Kuwait, whose defenses were overwhelmed quickly. The emir of Kuwait, his family, and other government leaders fled to Saudi Arabia immediately, and within hours Kuwait City had been captured, and our Iraqi forces established a provincial government.

And I knew exactly why.

With this successful takeover, Iraq would now control twenty percent of the world's oil reserves as well as substantial territory on the coastline of the Persian Gulf. That same day, I listened as reports came in that the United Nations Security Council denounced the invasion unanimously and demanded Iraq's immediate withdrawal from Kuwait.

In the following days, I watched the television and listened to the radio around the clock. Three days after the invasion, I received orders for a mission.

To fly to Kuwait.

I inquired as to who my passenger would be, but the information was not available for disclosure. I prepared the plane and waited, my mind racing. I had flown hundreds of missions in all kinds of conditions, but this was different. The invasion had begun a few days prior, and I had no idea what kind of conditions I would be flying into.

It wasn't long before three men strode toward the plane. They were all members of Iraqi intelligence, and by the looks on their faces, I knew they meant business. They nodded at me, and I nodded back. It was time to go.

"Be careful," my squadron leader said just before takeoff. "We've already had a couple of planes hit by Strelas. I don't want you to be one of them."

"Yes, sir," I said.

A Strela is a lightweight, shoulder-fired, surface-to-air missile system, designed to target aircraft at low altitudes and hit them with a high explosive warhead.

I took a deep breath and then pushed aside all thoughts of danger ahead. I couldn't allow fear or anxiety to plant and take root in my mind. I needed a clear head and quick reflexes.

The flight from Baghdad to Kuwait didn't take long. My pulse quickened with each passing minute as we neared the border. As soon as we passed into Kuwaiti airspace, I flew low to avoid rockets, ground-to-air missiles, and radar while keeping an eye out for Strelas. The ground appeared to be only an arm's reach away. And then suddenly, the airfield came into view.

My eyes scanned the area for a place to land. The runway was filled, and there was no empty space. The taxiing runway was empty. It was not designed for landing, but it was my only option.

I guided the plane down and we landed safely. As soon as we touched down, three vehicles sped toward the plane.

"Just wait for us here!" one of the members of the Iraqi intelligence team shouted as he exited. "We won't need longer than sixty to ninety minutes on the ground, and then we need to get back to Baghdad immediately."

I nodded.

They disappeared, and as soon as they were out of sight, I turned to my copilot.

"Stay here. I'm going to have a look around," I said.

Even from afar I could see damage caused by the invasion, and I wanted to get a better look. My copilot knew there was no stopping me and didn't even attempt to protest. He just nodded. There were at least seven other aircrafts parked beside ours. As I walked past, bullet holes in one of the Egyptian planes caught my eye—indicative of an eventful flight.

As I approached the terminal, a pit lodged in my stomach. It was pure chaos and carnage. I had been there just a couple of weeks before, and it was beautiful, clean, and whole. Now it was utterly destroyed.

All the windows of the international terminal were smashed. Shards of glass littered the walkways. It looked as if a tornado had ripped through the entire building. Important documents from the main offices had been thrown onto the floor, and I couldn't take a single step without trampling on them. There was not even an inch of bare floor visible.

The duty-free shop was a jungle, victim to the power-drunken whims of soldiers on a rampage. Every display case had been thoroughly raped, and the floor was littered with the aftermath. Rolex watches studded the wrists of every Iraqi soldier that I passed.

My stomach turned and my chest felt heavy.

Why? Why destroy everything? Why rape and pillage?

I felt ashamed of my fellow soldiers and the thoughtlessness of their actions. It was needless. This was more than just an invasion; this was a show of force. This was a broad smile on the bully's lips; this was a look of pleasure in the rapist's eyes. It wasn't necessary or strategic; it was barbaric and thoughtless.

I hated it.

I made my way to the tower to get a better look at the area. Again, it was filled with the remains of destructive acts. Runway lights had been destroyed. Instrument panels for radar and communications had been shattered by machine-gun fire. Anger rose up within me. This needless damage to property deeply bothered me. It was reckless, thoughtless, and in my eyes, without honor.

I left the tower and walked to the catering area. Iraqi forces had cut the power supply after the invasion. Caviar dotted the floor from the expensive jars that had been opened and discarded. The front of the industrial refrigerators looked like a cheese grater, full of bullet holes.

"You motherfuckers," I whispered. "How could you do this? What's the point? Why all the destruction? Are we in the 12th century? Are we fucking pirates?"

I was ashamed.

Ashamed that my fellow countrymen had so little honor and respect. Ashamed of the barbaric nature of their actions. I paced the hallways and corridors, taking in the sight of total destruction, and my chest felt heavy.

After a while, I checked the time. The intelligence team would be ready to leave soon, but I still had a few minutes to spare. I wanted to see the grand reception hall that had welcomed us on my last trip with Arafat. It wasn't far, and I knew I could make it there and back to the plane in enough time for takeoff.

I walked quickly, and soon the grand entrance came into view—that massive, beautiful door that I had admired just days before. But my heart sank as I stepped inside. The entire floor was flooded with water that smelled of sewer. Soldiers had clogged the toilets with T-shirts and created an overflow—another needless act of destruction. The power supply had been cut off, making it impossible to pump the water out. It sat in stagnation, stinking and seeping into every crack and crevice. The space had been so beautiful, so welcoming, so pristine. And now it was in shambles.

I had seen enough. I made my way back to the plane quickly and prepared for takeoff. My mind was still replaying the images of chaos and carnage I had just seen.

"What did you see? What happened?" my copilot asked as I busied myself with the preflight procedures.

"It's total chaos. Destruction." I spat the words with disgust. "I was just here, not even two weeks ago. Everything was perfect, orderly, and clean. So, to see it like this, needlessly pillaged and looted, it's maddening. There's no need to steal watches or smash jars of caviar. There's no need to ruin a perfectly good control tower. And to know that it's our countrymen responsible makes me sick. To attack is one thing. To take such pleasure and pride in it is another. I'm ashamed."

Within ten minutes the intelligence team returned to the aircraft, along with four other men who all loaded quickly into the plane. Once again, I stayed at a low level to keep us out of radar range and reduce the risk of being hit. I kept a sharp lookout for Strelas. Soon, the vast desert sand came into view. It was dotted with cars that had attempted to flee across the sand. There was no road, no proper pathways to travel on, and far too many vehicles lay stranded and broken down.

Once we crossed the border and were safely on Iraqi soil, I breathed a little easier. We landed safely in Baghdad, and the four new passengers exited, wearing a traditional Dishdasha thobe, an ankle-length white dress with long sleeves. I didn't know who they were, and I didn't ask. They were not the type of men one inquires about.

"Wait here," said one of the Iraqi intelligence members to me, just minutes after landing. "We need to return to Kuwait in just a few hours."

"Yes, sir," I said but inwardly questioned the order. In these types of situations, it was common practice to switch pilots after a long shift. Immediately, I searched for my squadron leader and explained the situation.

"Mohammed, they specifically requested you," my squadron leader said. "You are one of our best pilots and one of the only ones to land since the invasion. You know what you're getting into. Freshen up. It's got to be you."

I nodded.

My body was weary from stress and the ache of the things I had seen. But the moment I had my orders, my adrenaline kicked in and my mind went clear, my senses sharp. After about four hours, the same three Iraqi intelligence members appeared, along with the other four men, still dressed in their traditional Dishdasha thobe.

We took off again, and my vision became sharp. With each passing minute, my pulse thumped a little harder as we neared the border. I began the descent to prepare for a low flight path. I braced myself, ready and prepared for anything.

Soon the airfield came into view.

"Don't even shut off the engine when we land!" one of the Iraqi intelligence members shouted to me as we approached landing. "We're going to drop these three guys off and then get the hell out of here."

"Roger that," I said. I didn't want to spend any more time than necessary on the ground.

It was still impossible to land on the runway, just as I expected. I made a smooth landing on the taxi runway, and the three men dressed in white exited and made their way to a waiting vehicle, which sped away the moment they were inside.

"Let's go, let's go!" one of the team members shouted as the doors closed. Our mission was done.

I wasted no time in taking off, returning the way we came—low level and near the ground. I kept a sharp lookout for anything out of the ordinary, but nothing happened. Again, I breathed easier when we were safely within Iraqi airspace.

We landed safely in Bagdad and my body relaxed. But curiosity pushed and prodded the edges of my mind. I still had no idea what the nature of these two missions had been or who these men were.

The three Iraqi intelligence members didn't appear to be in a hurry. They took their time gathering their things, and I struck up a conversation with them as they walked past the cockpit. They were engaging and seemed happy to chat after the stressful day we had all experienced. They fiddled with the instruments and asked all kinds of questions about flying and being a pilot. I made casual conversation, but inwardly I was bursting to find out more about the two missions we had just carried out.

Ask them. Just ask them or you'll never know.

I gathered up the nerve and cleared my throat.

"Who were those guys?" I asked as the three men prepared to exit the plane.

I gauged their expressions to see if I had stepped over a line I wasn't supposed to. But they didn't miss a beat.

"That's the temporary Kuwaiti government that Saddam just put into place after the invasion," one of the men answered. "The flight earlier today was so that they could meet with Saddam."

Holy shit.

I prodded a bit more to try and get as many details as possible, but that was the only nugget of information I was going to receive it seemed.

I made my way back to my home, exhausted but still filled with angst about the entire situation. I showered and changed my clothes and then positioned myself in front of the television to watch the news. Within minutes, the screen flashed with a video of the three passengers that had been in my plane just hours before. One of them was shaking Saddam's hand. Their voices were inaudible, and music played in the background, but the voice of the reporter could be clearly heard. Saddam was shaking hands with the appointed leader of Kuwait.

I sat up straight.

I couldn't believe my eyes. I knew they were part of the new temporary government but had no idea that one of them was Saddam's newly appointed leader. To say my mission had been important would be a gross understatement. My stomach clenched in retrospective anxiety at the mission I had just carried out. I was grateful I hadn't been aware of it before.

The weeks that followed the Iraqi invasion of Kuwait were filled with tension and a disturbing awareness of the unknown. I continued to carry out orders I was given without question but something inside of me felt strange and uncomfortable. I was an amazing pilot, and I was performing my duties well. But I hated the heaviness in my chest that pressed in with the knowledge I was carrying out missions for a corrupt and brutal regime. I hated the violence and disregard for humanity. I hated the decisions Saddam was making on behalf of my country.

By August, Operation Desert Shield, the American defense of Saudi Arabia, began as US forces raced to the Persian Gulf. By this time, Saddam had built up the Iraqi occupying army to about 300,000 troops in Kuwait. It's hard to describe the tension we lived with daily as citizens—watching the situation unfold, being powerless to do anything about it.

In November, the United Nations Security Council passed a resolution authorizing the use of force against Iraq if it failed to withdraw by January. And it came as no surprise to any of us when Saddam refused to withdraw. He had already established a province of Iraq.

More than 700,000 allied troops, including 540,000 US personnel and smaller numbers of British, French, Egyptians, Saudis, Syrians, and several other national contingents gathered in the Middle East to enforce the deadline in response.

The situation was only escalating.

I lived with a constant sense of fear. It wrapped around my chest and squeezed tightly. I desperately wanted to see Saddam overthrown, to see Iraq freed from his viscous clutch. But none of us wanted to live in a war zone. I hated the fighting, the violence, the collateral damage that is an inevitable part of any military operation.

Over the next few weeks, the United States led the famous air campaign known as Operation Desert Storm and the sustained aerial bombardment that successfully destroyed Iraq's air defenses. I hated to see the destruction of such valuable equipment and beautiful machinery, but I understood the strategic importance of doing so on the part of the United States. In the following days, communications networks, government buildings, weapons plants, oil refineries, and bridges and roads were also attacked.

I could only hold my children tight and pray for a better future for them. One without such unrest and uncertainty, one without so much violence.

My heart sank when I learned Saddam had placed a bounty on the heads of British and American pilots enforcing the no-fly zones over Iraq. He promised approximately 30,000 dinars for taking down an enemy aircraft; 10,000 dinars for a live enemy pilot; and 5,000 dinars for a dead enemy pilot. That was enough money to make even decent men contemplate terrible deeds.

I thought of all the pilots who woke up every morning just as I did, following orders, doing as they were told. Weren't we all trying our best to do the right thing in a bad situation? Weren't we all just pieces in a massive chess game played by powerful people we would never even meet? Weren't we all lovers of the art of flight, captivated by the sky? And weren't we all hoping to make it home safely and kiss our sweethearts and tuck our children in bed just one more time?

I couldn't bear the thought of good and decent pilots being treated like prize slaughter pigs up for sale to earn a little cash. I couldn't bear the thought of good men and women being shot down or captured and inhumanly treated.

I couldn't stop this evil. I couldn't hold back the tidal wave. I didn't want to risk the safety of my family, but I couldn't sit by and not do anything.

I prepared a room in my house to be ready for any pilot who was gunned down or forced to make a crash landing on Iraqi soil. I kept an ear out constantly for any news of an aircraft being shot down or a pilot on the loose. I would be ready. Ready to provide safe refuge to any pilot who found themselves in that unthinkable situation. The one that all pilots fear most from the day we took flight.

I never had to use that room for this purpose. I listened and watched and waited. But the opportunity never came. Even still, I was ready. I hated the force of evil that Saddam's reign had brought upon my people. As such, I sympathized with the American cause.

Beyond that, I was first and foremost a pilot. I did my job with honor and dignity, and I respected any other pilot who did the same. To think of a fellow pilot being hunted down like animals, tortured, imprisoned, or killed was a thought I could not bear.

It is easy to forget the humanity of soldiers. To see only pieces and functions. But I never forgot that inside each plane that dotted the sky, there was a man or woman with a life. With hopes and dreams. With spouses and children. I knew there were plenty of assumptions that could be made about me in the position that I held. I was often at war with myself —battling between a love for my job and a hatred for the man I worked for.

And I desperately hoped that if I found myself in the wrong place at the wrong time someone would also have the courage to see the humanity in me.

CHAPTER EIGHT_

In early 1994, the time came for me to renew my yearly paperwork that was required for serving on the VIP squad. All of us dreaded it. "A colonoscopy of one's life" is the best way I can describe it. Every year we were handed a book, *a thick book,* and instructed to fill it out. Every question you can possibly imagine was listed there. If there was a section asking me to list every time I had ever had sex in my life, complete with which positions I had had it in, I wouldn't have been surprised.

They left no stone unturned. They wanted to know every detail about our lives, our family's lives, and the lives of our family's families. And we didn't dare lie. They would find out. One little mistruth, one little white lie would result in deep trouble. No matter how small, any untruth would be considered a complete breach of trust.

It was my seventh time to go through the process. Seven

years of submitting to the mandatory colonoscopy. It never got easier. And there was no way around it, only through it. So, I made myself comfortable, gritted my teeth, and began. When I got to the section about my extended family and my wife's extended family, I paused for a moment. There were lists of questions, asking where each member of the family currently lived. They were all questions I had filled out before. My hand began moving robotically across the page, mentally reciting the same answers I had always given. But when I got to the section about my wife's parents, I paused.

They had recently moved to the United States to be near my brother-in-law and sister-in-law, who had moved there years before to study at an American university. I listed their new location as well as all the details I had about their reasons for moving, job status, etc. I let out a sigh of relief when I finally completed the last page and handed over the book.

Thank goodness I don't have to touch that again for another year.

A few weeks later, I received an order to appear at the palace. I dressed in my uniform on the appointed day and showed up, just as instructed, expecting a quick bureaucratic meeting. But nothing could have prepared me for what was awaiting me. I was ushered into a small room and was greeted by an officer wearing an icy expression. The officer motioned to a chair on the other side of his desk, and I took a seat.

"Mohammed, it has come to our attention that certain members of your family have recently relocated to the United States, is that correct?" the officer asked. His eyes met mine, but his face remained expressionless.

An unsettling feeling washed over me. There was

something cold in the officer's eyes, something distant about the tone of his voice.

"Well, yes. In a manner of speaking, I suppose," I stammered, a bit surprised by the question. "My wife's parents recently relocated to the United States to be closer to my brother-in-law and sister-in-law, who have lived and studied there for quite some time."

The officer blinked in acknowledgment, his expression never changing.

"And have you ever shared confidential information regarding President Saddam Hussein or any other official members of the Iraqi government?" the officer asked.

I searched the officer's face for some hint that he was on my side, that I wasn't really being accused of passing along confidential information to the United States, that this was just routine questioning. But the officer's iron gaze gave me no sense of comfort.

"Of course not," I said, still shocked at how ludicrous the accusation sounded. "I would never do such a thing." My words sounded weak and meaningless. I was caught off guard. I had no defense prepared because I hadn't anticipated the attack. I tried to think fast, tried to form words that would make the officer believe me, make the officer understand I was nothing more than a simple pilot who loved his job and wanted to provide well for his wife and children.

"I have been a trusted member of the VIP squad for years. I am the son of General Adel, and I have never done a single thing that would compromise our government's security. I have no interest in politics or secrets or anything of that sort. I am just a pilot," I explained.

Even as I tasted the words on my lips and listened to the sound of my voice echo through the room, a deep sinking feeling washed over me. My words didn't even seem to register in the officer's eyes. Like a rubber band bouncing off an iron shield, not a word I said penetrated the officer's cold, hard expression.

And then it hit me.

Like a tidal wave.

Like a knife.

I was no longer on the VIP squad. I was being fired and there was nothing I could say or do that would change that fact.

"We cannot allow anyone who has family members living outside of Iraq to serve on the VIP squad. It is also still unclear to us whether or not you have been sharing confidential information with your US-based relatives. As such, your services are no longer needed on the VIP squadron," the officer said.

The words seemed to echo off the walls as they confirmed everything I feared. I was no longer on the inside. I was not just out; I was now under suspicion. After all the years I had spent devoting myself to the job, keeping quiet when I could have spoken, and striving to be the picture of professional discretion, I was pushed to the outside simply because my wife's parents decided to move to the United States.

I blinked with shock.

And then came the rage.

Anger boiled up from within as if it had been waiting for an opportunity to spew out.

"It's my wife's parents!" I suddenly spat out. "We are talking about MY WIFE'S PARENTS! I didn't move to the United States. I didn't trade secrets or expose confidential information. My in-laws moved to America. That's it. That's all that happened. And I'm suddenly out? Finished? Just like that?"

My voice shook with anger and rose to a higher pitch. "I am the son of General Adel! I am one of the top pilots on the squad! You can't just get rid of me like that."

"The decision is final," the officer said. His gaze was still as icy as it had been when I walked in.

My mind raced.

This can't be the end. This can't be the end.

But it was. No matter how many strategies I tried to clear my name or words I said to convince them otherwise, there was no changing the fact that I would never be allowed back on the VIP squad because my wife's Christian parents lived in the United States.

I felt bitter. Angry and bitter.

Since the time I was just a boy I had worked and applied myself to be the best pilot I possibly could be. Even when faced with piloting for horrible, brutal, stupid people, I kept my cool. Even when forced into impossible situations, I maintained ultimate grace and professionalism. And I was a good pilot. A *fucking good* pilot. I was one of the most requested pilots on the squad.

And now it was over.

All the prestige, all the honor, all of it was gone.

In the weeks that followed, my whole world was turned upside down. I had served on the VIP squad since graduation. It was all I knew. The whole situation felt wrong and unfair. But I was powerless to do anything about it.

In moments like these you realize that no matter how much power or prestige or reputation you feel you've earned, when you are at the mercy of an unfeeling governmental machine, nobody cares about the sacrifices you've made. Nobody remembers the times you held your tongue or chose to speak respectfully or devoted yourself entirely to the job. The moment you step over that line from being in to being out, everything changes.

At first, I fought. An anger boiled up in me that I didn't even know existed beneath my polite and passive surface. All the feelings I pushed down, all of the words I refused to speak, all of the mistreatment I tolerated had been with me all along. It had festered and grown beneath the lies I told myself to force another smile on my face and move forward.

I thought of every possible strategy to get someone to hear my side of the story and restore me to my former position. I tried every single one. I made phone calls, I pleaded, I coerced, I put my foot down, I asked. But no matter how hard I tried, nothing worked. My anger simmered down into an uncomfortable acceptance, and I began to search for another job.

But even the very process of job searching felt humiliating. There was nowhere to go but down after holding the type of position that I had. But I had to do something. I had a wife and family. I was still young. I couldn't sit on the sidelines and lick my wounds. I had to get back in the game.

After a few months, an opportunity arose for me to enroll in school to become a flight instructor.

Slowly, the realization set in that I would never be a VIP pilot again. Everything I had worked so hard to become, all the compromises I had made to keep my job seemed to be for nothing. I had no voice, no means of setting the record straight or clearing my name. The one thing I had devoted my life to had been snatched out of my hand in a matter of days. I had been wadded up like a paper napkin and disposed of.

I hated feeling powerless. I hated the knowledge that I was nothing more than a cockroach under the feet of an oppressive force. Suddenly, I wanted to fight. I wanted to shout and hear my own voice proclaiming all the things I had pushed down inside. I was furious with my government. I was afraid for what the future would hold for me and my family if we continued to live under the shadow of suspicion. We lived with daily reports of military attacks and political unrest. So, in the dark of night, my wife and I began to whisper the thing that we both were thinking.

Maybe we could get away.

Maybe we could start a new life for our children.

The whispers turned into action as we began to formulate a plan. We would escape to Jordan and then find a way to get to the United States.

The plan was far simpler for my wife than for me. My wife was free to travel and fly anywhere. But I was not. Though semi-retired, I was still technically a member of the Iraqi military, which meant I was not allowed to travel or fly without permission. I was already seen through a lens of distrust, my every movement under microscopic analysis. Any sudden or strange behaviors could have dire consequences.

In order to get to Jordan, I would have to forge documents under a fake name. It was the only strategy to get away. From there, we'd find a way to get into the United States. But I didn't want to start a new life with a fake identity. I didn't want to live with one eye always looking over my shoulder.

I told myself if I could just get to the United States, I could find someone whom I could talk to. I would tell them my identification was false and show them my real name, my credentials. I would prove I was a respected pilot. If anyone could help me, it had to be the Americans. The plan had flaws. Major ones. But I was angry and desperate. The greatest thing in life I cared about had been taken from me and I couldn't sit back and just let it happen. I didn't want to raise my children under oppression and constant fear. There was no future for my family in Iraq.

So I began to put our plan into action. I got false identification papers and arranged an off-book flight with one of my contacts from the Air Force. I told no one. Only in hushed moments did my wife and I speak of the thing we were about to do. We planned every detail, thought of every contingency, and finally, we had a day set for departure. Anything we didn't need we sold as subtly as possible so as not to attract attention.

My wife's and my children's tickets were scheduled a few days ahead of mine. I kissed them goodbye and promised I would join them soon in Jordan. I forced my voice to sound calm and confident as I spoke, but inwardly I felt unsettled.

There was no turning back at this point. We had sold everything. We had tied up every loose end. My wife's parents were waiting expectantly for her in the United States. I was ready for my children to start a new life away from the unrest in Baghdad. I was ready to sleep soundly at night without worrying for their safety. I wanted us all to have a better life than what would await us if we stayed in Iraq.

My wife called me shortly after landing in Jordan. Everything had gone like clockwork. I promised I would come as soon as I could. My flight was just a few days away, but the hours seemed to drag on. My mind was in a constant loop, wondering again and again if I had missed something. But everything was in order. Everything was just perfect.

Until a call came that changed everything. A call to inform me that my mother had died suddenly. I was stunned and shocked. I knew her health, both mental and physical, had not been well since my brother was killed, but I hadn't prepared myself for her death and certainly hadn't expected it just days before leaving.

I was torn between two unthinkable choices.

I needed to be on a plane to Jordan. But I couldn't leave while my father and brother grieved my mother's death without giving her a proper burial. She deserved more than that. My family had already grieved and suffered intensely after my brother's death, and I couldn't live with myself if I abandoned them in the midst of another loss.

With a heavy heart, I canceled my flight to Jordan. All the

work, all the coordination to make it anonymously across the border was destroyed. In the weeks that followed, I tried to save the sinking ship, tried to salvage the situation, but I couldn't. The stars never seemed to align again for me to leave the country.

When my wife and children returned to Iraq after our failed escape, it was as if the color had been drained from everything. We had prepared ourselves for starting a new life, we had dreamed of a new chapter, and we thought we were turning the page. Everything felt suddenly empty. I grieved the death of my mother amid that hollow void. I grieved the fact that her final years on earth were spent living in the pain and anguish of a tortured mind after my brother's brutal murder.

A slow acceptance crept in as the months passed. I began to think that maybe things would never change. Maybe this was all that life would bring us. I put everything I had into being the best flight instructor I possibly could. But something in me ached like pains from a slow death. I wanted to feel the freedom of the air. I wanted the thrill of receiving a mission and wondering who I'd be flying that day. After the risks I had taken to keep my job, after the abuse I had endured just to earn my place, I still couldn't believe it was all over.

But time has a way of cooling fiery resistance to what you dislike and don't want. The familiarity of routine, the monotony of rising each day to do the same tasks can lull even the strongest man into compliance.

The years following my mother's death and our failed escape attempt felt more like sleepwalking than living. My movements were mechanical and robotic. I embraced routine as a substitute for finding passion in my job or relationships. I was placed on semi-retired status, which didn't occupy my time like my former position had. I still provided for my family, and I maintained our house. Somehow one year turned into another and then another. But nothing could squelch my rage at the oppression of Saddam's brutal dictatorship. I would never stop resisting the raping of freedom I witnessed daily under Saddam's rule. Saddam's complete disregard for life and his severe violations of human rights sickened me.

No one can ever really know the total number of deaths and disappearances related to Saddam's savage repression, but many estimate it to be more than 250,000 people across his reign of terror, a great majority of which occurred as a result of the Anfal genocide in 1988 and the suppression of the uprisings in Iraq in 1991. We were surrounded with the constant reality of living with secret police, state terrorism, reports of hideous torture, mass murder, genocide, ethnic cleansing, rape, deportations, extrajudicial killings, forced disappearances, assassinations, and chemical warfare.

Every night as I saw the innocent peace of my children's sleeping faces, my soul ached. I longed for some assurance to cling to, some sure footing of knowing my children would be safe. But no such assurances existed for Iraqi parents during those hard years. We lived in fear. Constant, gnawing fear.

And that fear only escalated in the dawn of the early 2000s. I watched in shock and horror along with the rest of the world as reports of a plane hijacking and terrorist attack on the World Trade Center in New York City flooded the news channels. My stomach churched, and my hands shook with rage. I couldn't wrap my mind around that type of heartless brutality. And although Iraq had nothing to do with 9/11, the attacks in the United States changed everything in the lives of the Iraqis. The US invaded Afghanistan, overthrowing the Taliban regime that had been sheltering Osama bin Laden, the infamous leader of the al-Qaeda terror network blamed for the attacks, and then they swiftly shifted their attention to Iraq.

On March 17, 2003, President George W. Bush gave a speech that changed everything:

"Events in Iraq have now reached the final days of decision," he said in his address to the American people. "For more than a decade, the United States and other nations have pursued patient and honorable efforts to disarm the Iraqi regime without war. The regime has a history of reckless aggression in the Middle East. And it has aided, trained, and harbored terrorists, including operatives of al-Qaeda. The danger is clear: using chemical, biological or, one day, nuclear weapons, obtained with the help of Iraq, the terrorists could fulfill their stated ambitions and kill thousands or hundreds of thousands of innocent people in our country, or any other. Recognizing the threat to our country, the United States Congress voted overwhelmingly last year to support the use of force against Iraq."

This speech changed everything for the Iraqi people.

Both the United States and the United Kingdom claimed Saddam Hussein was developing weapons of mass destruction and that he presented a threat to his neighbors and to the world community. As such, the United States vowed to destroy Iraqi weapons of mass destruction and end the dictatorial rule of

Saddam Hussein. And for the first time in a long time, those of us who had been living under the oppressive reality of Saddam's regime felt something we hadn't in a long time. We felt hope.

Hope that the heavy hand of brutality could be overpowered and destroyed, hope that we could create a safer and better world for our children. For years we had been powerless to stand up and push back against the evil that held us down. We had no power, no means to fight the oppression that pushed against our backs until we could hardly breathe. Maybe with the United States on our side, things would be different.

But still, we braced ourselves for the worst. The future was unclear and unpredictable. There is no way to prepare for the impact of an invasion, for war in your own backyard. We could not anticipate the impact nor the implication of the dominoes that began to fall in early 2003. I craved freedom and a better future for my nation but dreaded the certain collateral damage that would come with war in my territory. More than anything, I hated that my children were stuck in the middle of it all. Young minds and bodies should never have to live with constant fear or the trauma of war.

By summer of 2003, life had changed drastically for local Iraqis. The sounds, smells, and visions of war surrounded us. There was no escaping it. My family remained healthy and untouched, but never did I have even a moment's relief from the constant fear that strangled me as I worried for their safety.

The United States quickly gained control, but the very cunning Saddam disappeared. And the hunt was on. Even without holding a position of public power, the fact that he was still out there somewhere gave me an uncomfortable feeling that I couldn't shake. Finally, in December of 2003, reports of Saddam's capture flooded media outlets around the world. I stared at the pictures of a disheveled shell of a man pulled from the ground and could hardly believe that it was the same man I had flown countless times. The powerful dictator in a pressed uniform had been exchanged for a wild-haired, crazed man in rags. I could still hear Saddam's voice in my ear, feel the weight of Saddam's palm on my shoulder, see the images of Saddam seated in my plane, waiting for takeoff.

I saw the humanity of the man. I saw Saddam crouched over and naked as he changed his clothes. I saw him laugh and smile in private. I saw him hungry and thirsty. I heard Saddam thank me for my service and call me son. Somewhere inside the monster of the man, a human still existed. I saw it with my own eyes.

But it only made me hate him more. How a man could be capable of inflicting such atrocities on his fellow humans was something I could never understand. To see and touch evilness bottled inside of human flesh, skin, and bones is an experience I will never fully be able to wrap my mind around.

And by the time I saw the remains of the man retrieved from that underground hole, it was obvious the shreds of humanity that Saddam maintained had eroded away. I couldn't help but think it must be exhausting for a body to hold all that evil inside. It must be a weight felt through every muscle and joint, like an infection eating him from the inside out—a slow death to sound thought and able body.

The knowledge that Saddam was in custody made me breathe easier but still offered no relief from the constant worry that bore down on me as a father trying to raise his children in the midst of a war. As a parent, you bear the responsibility of protecting another human's life. You are entrusted with the care of small minds, souls, and bodies, and it is a weight that cannot be lifted. We all hoped and prayed that the American invasion would bring about a peaceful new chapter for Iraq, but the future was unclear, and the path to get there was full of danger and uncertainty. We were chess pieces in a game played by men in high places. A game that the world watched from above, never fully seeing the reality of how it impacted good families like mine.

In early 2004, my wife received a phone call from her parents. They wanted her and the children to move to the United States and live in Michigan with them. They had been working on the details for a while, and it seemed they had finally found a way. All at once I felt relief and a sense of deep sadness. I felt relief at the idea of knowing that my children would be safe, that I wouldn't have to worry every night about whether they would become collateral damage in a game outside my control. And then I felt deep sadness with the knowledge that I could not join them in the United States yet. I had tried. I needed to keep my job, keep supporting my family, and keep trying to find a way.

The day I said goodbye to my children was one of the hardest days of my life. I knew the reality of the situation. I knew it would likely be years before I would be able to join them. I knew I would miss out on watching them grow through childhood stages, miss listening to them talk and laugh, miss seeing those arms around my neck as they hugged me tight.

I watched as they packed their suitcases, looks of innocent delight on their faces. My oldest daughter, Rania, was eighteen; my second daughter, Rand, was sixteen; my son Rami was eleven; and my youngest daughter, Rula, was only four. They didn't know what was ahead. They were about to arrive in a foreign country without speaking the language, with little understanding of the culture and customs. They had a long road ahead. I knew my older daughters would have to work hard to overcome the language barrier. High school is already a difficult time without being a foreigner in a new country. The younger children were too young to really understand what was happening. They would adapt, but it would be hard.

But they would be safe. *They would have a future.*

And that's all that mattered.

As I pulled each of them tight to my chest before saying goodbye, my soul ached with longing. I held them for as long as I could, feeling the rise and fall of breath between us, inhaling the scent of their nearness, wishing with everything in me that I could make time stop. I forced a smile to my lips. Forced myself to tell them that everything would be okay, that this was all for the best, to look calm and confident. But my soul bled that day.

Saying goodbye to a child to ensure a better future is an acute pain that I wouldn't wish upon my worst enemy. I felt the ache of it with every ounce of my being. An ache so deep that it was hard to even take in a full breath. But I didn't let them see my break. I kept my smile strong.

It's for the best.

It's for the best.

It's for the best. God, I hope this is for the best.

CHAPTER NINE_

The first few months after the departure of my wife and children were difficult. There was an unmistakable void that could not be filled with anything else. I spoke with them as often as I could, but there was no way around the cold reality that I did not live with them. I didn't live in the same home, city, or even country. I could not be there for them when they needed something, when things got hard.

The transition process from Iraq to the United States was tough on my family. They didn't speak the language and found it difficult to communicate and assimilate. The children went to an all-English-speaking school, and it proved to be a struggle. They could not understand the teachers or their fellow students. How could they be expected to learn when they couldn't even grasp the basics of human communication? They all shared one thick dictionary and would take turns huddled over it at night when school and work was done, straining to learn new words, to finish homework assignments. It was an uphill battle at every turn.

I knew that late night tears were being shed, that moving to a new country and having to completely start over seemed like too much to handle. But my wife and I knew that even all these challenges were a small price to pay for the peace of knowing our children were safe and had a better future ahead of them.

In December of 2004, I was placed on active duty again for the Iraqi Air Force. I applied for a new position to become an aerodynamics and flight safety instructor. I needed a new chapter—something to occupy my mind and my time. I was elated when I was accepted into the program. I completed a five-month training course in Jordan and then returned to Baghdad to assume my new position.

I enjoyed teaching. I devoted all my attention into being the best teacher I could. I pushed myself to learn as much as possible to find effective ways to communicate the information. It felt good to have a new challenge. It felt good to wake up with purpose. It was something to take my mind off the war raging in my backyard and the fact I was so far from my family. I tried to stay current with their day-to-day lives as much as possible, but it was hard to do across different countries and time zones. We all fell into new rhythms and routines without each other. Enough time can make even the strangest circumstances seem normal after a while. I hated that.

But family was not the only thing on my mind. It was difficult to live with the reality of war. I hated the loss of life, the destruction, the chaos, and the conflict it created. I just wanted peace, wanted to be near my children, wanted to lay my head on the pillow at night and know that everyone I loved was safe. I think that must be what the majority of men and women who fought during those difficult years felt. We all just wanted to live another day, to hug and kiss our children, to see evil abolished.

I tried to keep my head down and my mind busy, to make the time pass as fast as possible. Routine was a lifeline that I clung to for dear life. I forced a smile to my face, forced myself to keep my mind sharp and positive. There was no other way. I knew the moment I allowed a single crack, a break in my strong exterior, I would be risking the entire dam breaking and everything I had suppressed unleashing like a flood.

Somehow the months passed. And then a year. I was able to visit my family only once during that time. And that hurt.

In December of 2005, I received word about a two-week training course in the United States. My heart leapt when I saw the location. Maybe, just maybe, I would find a way to see my family for the Christmas holiday. My visa allowed me into the US for the training course, and it would still be valid at the time of my arrival. But getting through the US borders is never a certain thing. I would be intentionally staying long after my training ended to see my family. How border control would react to this fact I had no idea. There was always a chance I would show up and be turned away. To even hope was to play the lottery with a broken heart. I couldn't risk breaking my family's heart, so I didn't breathe a word about my trip to them. I couldn't give false hopes to them to hold on to only to have it ripped from their hands. If I must be refused at the border and return to Iraq without seeing them, I would bear that pain alone.

I packed my bags and booked a ticket to the United States. The hours in that plane seat dragged by. All those long hours I played one scene in my mind over and over like a movie on replay. The children running toward me. Faces of surprise and screams of joy when they realized their father had come home. Arms around my neck. Piles of arms and legs intertwined in happy reunion. I could feel them getting closer and closer. I wanted it. I *needed* it.

I forced a relaxed smile on my face as I approached the woman behind the desk at the immigration office.

Please let me pass. Please let me pass.

I presented my documents, and the immigration officer looked over them carefully. Silence hung in the air, my heart and hope in this woman's hands.

"What is the purpose of your stay here, Mr. Sulaiman?" the immigration officer asked.

This was the moment of truth.

"I'm a pilot, and I'm here for a training course. But my family lives in Michigan, and I am trying to surprise them for Christmas. I haven't seen them in almost a year," I said.

"Do you have any credentials or identification on you?" the immigration officer asked.

I produced my card and showed it to the officer. She looked over it and then again at my passport and visa. She then took a breath.

Her eyes met mine.

She could see it.

The desperate eyes of a father, the face of a man who would do anything just to have a chance to hold his family close.

She handed my documents back to me.

"Go surprise your family for Christmas," she said.

My ears had never heard a sweeter sound. If it weren't for security, I would have come around that desk and picked the immigration officer up and hugged her. Joy rose and anticipation swirled in my belly.

"Thank you so much," I said. I couldn't express my gratitude adequately with my words, but I could tell by the look in the immigration officer's eyes that she understood.

I grabbed my bags and took off. I couldn't make my connecting flight come any faster, but somehow, I felt like I needed to run to that gate. I had been given an open door, and I couldn't walk through it fast enough.

"Mr. Sulaiman, Mr. Sulaiman, wait, wait!" A voice brought me to a stop as I strode down the hallway.

I turned to see the woman from the immigration desk running in my direction.

Oh shit.

My chest clenched.

"Mr. Sulaiman, you forgot this," the immigration officer said, still breathing heavily.

In her hand was my passport and travel documents. In my joy and rush, I had forgotten them at the desk.

"You just saved my life," I said as immigration officer handed them over.

My heart began to thump when I landed in the Detroit airport. Every moment brought me a step closer. I hailed a taxi and threw my suitcases inside. My wife's home was several hours away in a city in Michigan. I didn't have an exact address for it, but I couldn't spoil the surprise by asking. But I remembered the basic directions for how to get there.

"If you can get me to the local Home Depot, I can direct you from there," I said.

The taxi driver nodded.

"What brings you to Michigan?" he asked.

I grinned and told him everything. Told him about having to say goodbye to my wife and children and living in different parts of the world. Told him of the Christmas surprise I was attempting to pull off.

His eyes were wide with wonder and happiness. Suddenly he was a part of the grand caper. When the Home Depot sign came into view, I could hardly contain my excitement. I sat up straight and began to direct the taxi driver toward the house. It was nearly midnight and pitch-black outside. With every turn, my heart thumped louder and louder.

And then my wife's house came into view.

"That's it!" I nearly shouted.

There were still lights on in the living room. It meant they were awake. Suddenly, my heart ached. I needed to hold them.

I grabbed my bags as fast as I could and began to walk to the door. I threw a glance over my shoulder toward the taxi driver, who was just standing there, staring at me.

"Everything okay?" I asked.

"Sure!" he yelled back. "I just want to see the surprise if that's okay."

I laughed. "Of course!"

Everyone was cheering for our reunion.

I rang the doorbell and waited.

One breath. Two breaths.

Footsteps.

Hands fumbling with the knob.

My wife opened the door and stared at me in shock for a split second, trying to comprehend what she was seeing. And then came the scream. In a second the entire house was filled with the sound of screams as everyone became the tangled pile of reunited hugging that I had dreamed of. I inhaled their nearness. Tears spilled from my eyes. All those months of suppressed emotions suddenly broke through the surface and spilled out in salty drops. I pulled back from the embrace to see their eyes. Their faces mirrored mine. Tears streamed, expressing all the things we couldn't find a voice to say, telling all the stories we couldn't tell all at once.

"Good luck!" the taxi driver called from his vantage point on the road. His face was beaming.

The two weeks I got to spend with my family that Christmas was a precious gift I'll never forget. I couldn't laugh enough, couldn't listen enough, couldn't hug enough, couldn't bottle up enough of the joy of being together to take with me.

An indescribable sadness came over me as I held my family close and said goodbye. I desperately wished I could find a way to make the space disappear between us. The time I had with them was no substitute for spending a life. But it was something and I had to be grateful for it. I clung to the hope that someday I would come and stay for good.

A deep melancholy washed over me as I settled into my

seat for the long flight from Detroit to Amman, Jordan. I closed my eyes, but sleep didn't come. A small child began to wail in the seat behind me, filling every corner of the plane with howls and sobs. An hour passed and then another. The cries never stopped. On and on they went. For a moment, blessed silence would come, and it seemed as if the entire plane was holding its breath, not moving for fear it would reactivate the tears. And just like clockwork, a fresh wave of sobs would come as if the silence had only provided new energy to create a fresh wave of tears. The hours seemed to drag on. The knowledge that I would not see my family again for a long time made my chest feel heavy. My mind grew weary, and my head pounded, every fresh wave of wails like an ice pick on my temples. I felt like a prisoner waiting for release as the plane descended into Amman. I needed silence. Desperately.

Even the din of the airport seemed like a blessed peace compared to the torture of listening to a screaming child for eleven hours straight. It would be another nine hours from Amman to Baghdad, and I already dreaded the long trip. I wasted no time in grabbing my luggage and finding a driver to take me to Baghdad.

A woman rushed toward the car as I loaded my luggage inside.

"Are you going to Baghdad?" she asked. "My son and I are going as well. Can we please share your vehicle?"

She seemed like a nice woman, and I wanted to be kind. But then I noticed the small child holding her hand. The little boy was barely two years old and stared up at me with an unreadable expression on his face. My ears still echoed with the phantom screams of that monstrous child aboard the plane. I had just endured eleven hours of torture. My mental sanity would not bear another nine hours of screaming.

I looked at the little boy, who buried his face in his mother's leg as he held tight to her hand.

You're another little screamer, aren't you? Just a ticking time bomb. Ten minutes in the car and I bet you'll make it your mission to make my life miserable.

I sighed.

I wanted to be a good person. And that meant not murdering anyone due to a mental breakdown.

"Why don't you take this vehicle," I said graciously. "You and your son have a safe trip back, and I'll find another car to take me."

"Oh, you're so wonderful," she gushed. "Thank you so much."

She overcalculated my level of chivalry, but I still nodded and helped her and her son into the car and waved them off. It didn't take long for me to find another driver and begin the long car ride to Baghdad. The ride was peaceful. I hit it off with the driver quickly, and we felt like old friends within minutes. We stopped for a few cold drinks and snacks and passed the time talking and laughing and watching the open road go by.

After several hours, as we approached the town of Anbar, I noticed commotion on the road. Several cars were parked at odd angles and the drivers had jumped out and were running ahead. I strained my eyes to get a better look. And then I saw it. A car overturned from a collision with a massive truck and trailer.

"Stop the car!" I yelled.

As soon as the driver threw on the brakes, I jumped from the vehicle and began to run. A few others were gathered around, and the moment I was close enough to read the expressions on their faces, my stomach clenched. I couldn't see what they were seeing, but I could see the horror registering in their eyes and draining the color from their faces. With shock, I realized that everyone was staring at the same vehicle I had given to the mother and son at the airport just a few hours earlier.

And then I saw it.

Both the mother and small child were dead.

Suddenly, I felt sick. The same woman I had just spoken with and the same little boy who had hugged her leg were now dead. All the hopes, dreams, and plans they had just ended in an instant.

And then another thought plunged into me like a knife:

I should have been in that vehicle. It should be my body lying on the pavement right now.

I sat in stunned silence, feeling my heart pound and my lungs rise and fall with rapid breaths.

I was alive.

I was alive when I should have been dead.

When it was clear there was nothing more that could be done, I climbed back into my vehicle, and we began to drive in somber silence. What can be said after seeing something like that?

I should be dead right now. I should be dead right now.

That thought set off a fast domino effect in my mind. I

should have died that day. But I didn't. Because of that screaming child on the plane and my thin nerves, I didn't accept that vehicle. I was still alive because of it.

And suddenly I realized I very much wanted to be alive.

It's not that I ever wanted to die. But through those hard years of being without my family, I had lost touch with a passion for life. I had become numb and desensitized, robotic and mechanical. And somehow looking death in the face brought me back to life. It reawakened the parts of me that had gone dormant. I felt things I hadn't felt in a long time. I felt deep gratitude for life. I felt passion pulse through me.

I had been given a gift. I had been given a new beginning. And I would make the most of it.

For the first time in a long time, I really *wanted* to live.

But what I did not realize was that my will to live would be tested in the following months.

CHAPTER TEN_

I began the new year of January 2006 with a renewed sense of purpose in life. All my senses were awake, passion alive. For the first time in a long time, I really wanted to live, I wanted to make a life I could be proud of. The mechanical numbness I had learned to exist with gave way to something I hadn't felt in a long time—hope, feeling, and a connection to life.

I invested all my mental energy into my job. I began to work more closely with the US military as the Iraqi Air Force was under the strict direction of the United States and made strong connections with many of the American men and women I met during that time.

As often as possible I would check on my family but was constantly aware of the fact that I did not live in close proximity to them. It was a sinking feeling for me to know I was missing so many years of my children's childhood. I wanted to hear their stories after school. I wanted to watch them grow every inch taller. I wanted to know I could be there at a moment's notice if necessary.

I tried to keep in contact as much as possible, but as time passed, even that was hard to do. They were creating an entirely new life without me. But that's how it had to be. They needed to make a home for themselves, find a new sense of normal. So I worked as much as possible.

On one particular day, I came home exhausted from work. I was tired, and I knew I would be returning home to an empty house once again. Loneliness can bring forth a specific type of lethargy that cannot easily be described. I made plans in my mind for what I would eat, trying to distract myself from the knowledge that it would be another long, quiet evening. I opened my front door, unsurprised by the silence that greeted me. But something else caught my attention.

An unmarked envelope was on the floor beneath my feet. I snatched it up immediately and tore it open. As my eyes scanned the words and their meaning registered in my mind, fear began to spread through me like a viral disease.

It was a death threat.

In just a few sentences, the message was clear. I should stop working with the Americans or my life would be in danger. My heart pounded as I took a seat on my sofa and tried to comprehend what I was reading. From all the wording, it appeared to be from al-Qaeda. It was the most obvious conclusion. But as I sat on my sofa another theory began to form in my mind.

Over the course of the last few years, Iran had carried out a systematic elimination of Iraqi pilots as a form of retaliation. In the aftermath of the invasion, Iran used the chaos to settle scores from the bloody Iran-Iraq war. The methods of warfare had been brutal—using poison gas, human wave, and bayonet attacks—and Iran was taking a special revenge on the pilots of the Iraqi Air Force. The revenge had caused my brother to lose his life and die an agonizing death. And since the collapse of Saddam's regime, the attacks had only grown more aggressive and more targeted.

Just a few months before, I watched the news in horror as reports that thirty-six pilots were gunned down in a largely Shiite neighborhood in the holy month of Ramadan. Numerous others had gone missing or been found dead. But listening to reports and reading articles about it was one thing. Finding a death threat under my own door was another.

I struggled to sleep that night. I didn't want to stay in my home, but I also had nowhere to go. And even if I did, I knew it wouldn't keep me safe. Whether it was al-Qaeda or Iranian Intelligence, it made no difference. If I was holding a death threat in my hand, then they already knew everything. They knew who I was. They had already been watching my every move. They knew about my trip to the United States. They knew my friends; they knew every member of my family.

There was nowhere to run, nowhere to hide. And so, I laid in my bed with full assurance that I was not safe.

The next day I got up with the first hints of light in the sky. I felt more tired from the night of restless attempts to sleep than when I had laid down. I dressed and drove to a US military base to explain the situation. I knew I was in over my head. I needed help. I needed protection. I needed backup. I was no match for the overwhelming force of evil that was stalking me. This was so much bigger than I was.

I brought the letter and explained the situation to my superiors. Once the words were spoken, I felt a sense of relief. They would form a plan and tell me what to do. I wouldn't be alone. But that relief was short-lived. I was met with a polite sympathy and an unmoved expression. They were sorry, but there was nothing they could do. This wasn't their problem or jurisdiction, they told me, and sent me to talk to the Iraqi Air Force. There wasn't even an ounce of room to ask for more or keep pressing. Their *no* was direct and firm.

I drove to another Air Force base where I had connections and once again explained my situation. But I was met with the same cold sympathy. After all I had given to the Iraqi military, after all I had sacrificed, it was hard to believe they wouldn't even attempt to help me. But the answer was clear. They weren't going to do anything.

I had no one else to turn to. No one else to ask for help and nothing else to do. In one way, my life was scary and surreal with the knowledge that someone wanted me dead, and, in another way, everything felt strangely ordinary and quiet. I continued to wake up every day and go to work. I came home each night and ate dinner with the television on and then rolled into my bed and tried to sleep. Only in the rare moments that I slipped into sleep did I escape that gnawing sense of dread, the paralyzing fear of being watched and hunted.

A week passed, then two, then three. Everything remained quiet and eerily unchanged.

Until it happened again.

Another envelope greeted me under my door. I tore it open and scanned it wildly, trying to take in every word at once. It was another threat. But it was stronger, more menacing, more forceful. The language left no room for questioning. The hands around my neck were squeezing tighter and tighter, and I couldn't catch my breath.

Another sleepless night passed with that letter in my home, screaming silent threats from the printed paper. I couldn't die like this. Anticipating my own death like a fool, helpless to do anything to save myself. I closed my eyes and pictured the faces of my children, trying to recall their scent when I pulled them close for one last hug before I left for the airport.

That can't be the last time I see my children.

This can't be the end.

I rose again the next morning and went straight to the US military base.

This time they would understand. I would *make* them understand.

My life was on the line, and I had nowhere to turn and nowhere to hide. Any sudden movements would only ignite the hunger of the evil beast more. I needed help, and I needed refuge.

But even with two death threats in hand, even with pleading and begging, they would not budge an inch on their position. This was a problem for the Iraqi Air Force, they told me. They would not, under any circumstances, get involved.

I returned to the Iraqi Air Force base and presented the second letter. But the answer was still the same. There was nothing they would do to help me. My words could not penetrate that cold wall of indifference.

"You're going to have to figure out a way to protect yourself. We cannot get involved," they said.

With those words spoken, I realized I was completely and utterly alone.

In the scope of this global game, I was not a father, a husband, or a son. I was a useless pawn in a worldwide chess match. My life meant nothing in the greater strategies being carried out. I was in the chaos between the tensions of Iran, Iraq, and the United States, and no one was coming to save me.

To be reduced to nothing more than a human chess piece is an unsettling reality. I could be tossed aside in an instant and no one would notice. I didn't know who to turn to. I had exhausted every option. No one wanted to help me; no one wanted to come to my aid.

How was I supposed to protect myself from a force of evil so unseen, so incalculable? There was an enemy that wanted me dead and had every means to do it. No matter where I went, they would know. I was out in the open, exposed, and vulnerable.

There was nothing to do but wait. To rise each morning, drink my coffee, and drive to work. To come home and eat and try to sleep. The only alternative was to run. And the moment I took that first step, there would be no turning back. It would mean saying goodbye to my home, my job, my reputation. I would lose everything.

And so, I waited. I stared into the barrel of the gun, trying not to flinch, not to run, not to make any sudden movements, hoping to God that it would pass.

But it didn't.

In April, I came home to find yet another envelope. This time it wasn't just a threat inside but a death certificate. And my name was written there neatly, cleanly. As if my death was already finalized, already certain. The hands were squeezing tighter and tighter around my neck, and I felt the oxygen draining from me. I made more attempts to get help from the American and Iraqi military without success. Every day felt like a slow march toward my own death.

The threats and certificates taunted me, screamed at me from where they lay in my house, an ever-present reminder that I was never really safe.

A few weeks later came the year's first taste of summer. The air was hot and heavy, and it pressed in relentlessly from every side. At the end of the day, I let myself into my home and searched for relief. I was thirsty and tired. I wanted something cool and refreshing. But my supply of ice had run out, and I couldn't bear the thought of sitting at home alone sipping a lukewarm drink. It was almost 5:00 p.m., which was curfew time across the city. The stores were closed, and I knew I should stay at home. But I figured that no one would notice if I went to my neighbor's house across the street in search of ice. So I threw on my shoes.

"Come in, come in!" My friend's wife greeted me with a smile when I knocked on the door.

"Please, please," I said, "I don't want to bother you. I am just looking for some ice. Mind if I borrow some?"

"No, no, no," she said. "You will stay for dinner. I insist. I am preparing food right now. Sit, drink, and relax."

She was not going to take no for an answer, and I was craving some good food and conversation to take my mind away from my anxious thoughts.

The cold liquid poured down my throat, and my senses seemed to awaken. My friend casually talked and laughed, and as I listened, I felt my shoulders relax just a bit. For just a moment, I didn't feel like I was in the middle of a war zone or under a death threat. I was just a man having drinks with my neighbor after a long day of work. And it felt good.

But at 7:00 p.m., just as the sun was beginning to set, sudden movement caught my attention from outside the window. Two pickup trucks barreled into view right in front of my house across the street and pulled to a stop. Several men jumped out with guns in hand.

The air exploded with the sound of rapid-fire gunshots. A torrent of bullets tore through my house. I stood in horror and shock. I couldn't find words to speak. Like a slow-motion movie, I witnessed what should have been my death. After a rainstorm of constant fire came total silence. The men appeared again, hopped the fence, climbed inside the waiting trucks, and then disappeared down the road.

Numb terror coursed through me. This was no longer a threat; it was now a reality. This was a full assassination attempt targeted directly at me. They knew there was a curfew, and they knew I would be inside my house, defenseless against the attack. I should be lying on the floor of my home with bullet-shredded flesh, bleeding out. I should be dying alone, wishing I could say goodbye to my wife and children.

But I wasn't.

I was standing safely behind a windowpane watching my assassination unfold in slow motion before my eyes.

All because I wanted some ice.

I stood there for several moments, my mind rushing into overdrive. The situation had now escalated to an entirely new level. It was time to make a plan.

I grabbed my phone and ran out of my neighbor's house and onto the street. I paused for a while and surveyed the area. I already knew the trucks were gone, but an uncomfortable sense of danger still hung in the air. The streets were silent. Not a single movement or sound. Everyone was locked inside their home because of the curfew, and the men and trucks had disappeared.

I walked to my front door and braced myself as I turned the handle.

The sight before me was even worse than I had expected. Hundreds of bullets had devastated the walls, the furniture, almost everything of value. I saw a flash of my own body, lying on the ground, seeped in red. I blinked away the image.

The time for waiting was over.

It was time to run.

CHAPTER ELEVEN_

I grabbed the phone from my pocket and began to snap pictures of the rooms. The bullet holes, the carnage, the proof. Then I left. I jumped into my car and drove directly to the American military base. Now I had evidence. I could show them everything I had said was true—all the letters, threats, and death certificates. They wanted me dead because of my involvement with the American military, and it was clear they would stop at nothing to finish the job.

As soon as I arrived on the military base, I went directly to one of the majors that I had become friends with. He was also a pilot, and we had formed a connection over the past several months. He was the only one I could think of to turn to. I told him everything. I scrolled through the pictures on my phone and showed them to him. My heart pounded, and my face felt hot. I could no longer hide my fear.

"I'm scared," I said, looking my friend in the eye, owning every word I said. "I'm really scared."

My friend drew in a long breath and then stared right back at me.

"Mohammed, what are you doing here?"

I searched my friend's face for understanding.

"You can't stay here. It's clear these people want you dead. And it's clear they will do anything to make sure and get the job done. At this point I don't think that anyone can keep you safe. It's time that you left town, Mohammed."

We looked at each other, and then I nodded my head. My friend was right. I couldn't fight this on my own, and no one was coming to my aid. Even if they did, it would likely be ineffective. I couldn't live my life in fear. I couldn't live my life hiding, hoping no one noticed I was still alive.

There was nothing more to say.

I shook my friend's hand, thanked him, and left.

I drove back to my house, parked outside, and searched the area for a few moments. No movement, no sound. My assailants had no reason to believe I wasn't dead, and it was unlikely they would return on the same night. I exited the car and slipped back into my house.

Even in the darkness, I could still see the mangled walls and floor littered with bullets. My home no longer felt familiar. The place I came to rest my head, to find peace and safety from the outside world, was now both hostile and somehow hollow. Every room felt sad, empty, and too quiet. Even the shadows didn't move. At that moment I realized I no longer had a home.

I was a fugitive. I was starting over. And nothing would ever be the same again.

I grabbed my passport and a few necessities, threw them in a backpack, and flung it over my shoulder. Everything else would have to stay behind. I paused for just a moment and scanned the home before flipping out the lights—an unceremonious goodbye to the life I had built.

I drove to my father's home and stayed the night, but sleep didn't come. I rehearsed my plan over and over in my mind, as if my imagination could force it into existence.

Airport...Baghdad to Jordan...Jordan to the United States...Then beg to stay.

Airport...Baghdad to Jordan...Jordan to the United States...Then beg to stay.

Airport...Baghdad to Jordan...Jordan to the United States...Then beg to stay.

There were hundreds of flaws in the plan. Hundreds of things that could go wrong. I could be refused at the border. I could be held for questioning. I could be misunderstood. But none of that mattered. It was all better than dying.

My heart humped steadily with unreleased anxiety as I boarded the plane. The flight from Baghdad to Jordan took only ninety minutes. I proceeded straight to border control, forcing myself to look calm and collected. I presented my documents to the border control officer and hardly let out a breath as he looked at them. One moment passed, then another, then another.

My stomach twisted. Something was wrong.

"Sir, if you can please step to the side."

Those were the words I dreaded hearing the most. I stepped aside without question and was escorted to a private room. My bags were taken from me, and they began a thorough search.

My heart sank.

Sure enough, they found what I tried to hide: my collection of identification cards. I had one for the Iraqi Air Force, another one for Iraqi Airlines, another one for the Jordanian Air Force that I received during one of my training programs. It created a confusing picture as to who I was and what I was doing on a flight to the United States. I wasn't even allowed to travel outside of Iraq.

The faces that stared at me were hard with skepticism and judgment.

One man leaned forward. It was obvious he would be the one asking questions.

"Just who are you, Mr. Sulaiman?" the man asked, as his eyes narrowed coldly. "And what are you doing with so many identification cards?"

I didn't want to begin with a lie. Once told, there would be no going back. Untruths are slippery, hard to hold on to. One mistake and everything shatters.

So I told them the truth. The entire truth. I told them about my history, prior job descriptions, and training as an explanation for the numerous identification cards in my possession. I told them about the death threats, about trying to flee the country. But the expressions did not soften or register a sense of understanding. With every word, I could feel their skepticism deepen, but I had nothing but the truth to say.

And they didn't believe a word of it.

I was escorted from the first room to another. There I was questioned again by another man. They pushed, they coerced, they insulted. They were looking for the crack in my story, the vulnerable place to hammer until breaking. I stuck to my story, which was easy to do because it was true. But even after two hours of talking, explaining, and begging, they still didn't believe it.

They took me to another room and questioned me for a third time. The hours dragged on. I checked the time and realized eight hours had passed. My eyes felt gritty and dry and every joint achy and fatigued. I'd hardly slept in days, and the constant anxiety had left me feeling pulled thin like a rubber band.

But they paid no mind to my exhaustion. Another round of questioning. Another stark room with bright lights. Even the tone of my own voice began to sound strange to my ears.

Ten hours.

Twelve hours.

Fourteen hours.

My legs and arms felt like lead. My mind became foggy and unfocused. At some point, I almost stopped caring altogether. I just wanted a bed. I just wanted a hot meal. I just wanted a shower. Even the knowledge that my life and future were on the line couldn't stop my bodily needs from shouting.

They asked the same questions, and I gave the same answers. Over and over and over until I felt as if I would scream or lose my mind. We were at a stalemate. They wouldn't believe my story, and I had nothing but the truth to offer. I searched my tired mind for a solution, someway forward. Going back would mean death. I was all in at this point.

"Can I make one phone call?" I asked. I had an idea and could only hope that it would work.

"One call," the man in front of me said after a pause.

I dialed the number of one of my father's friends—an Iraqi general in charge of Jordanian intelligence. The phone rang once, and I held my breath. It was now 4:00 a.m., and he would undoubtedly be asleep.

Please wake up.

Please wake up.

Please wake up.

It rang again.

"Hello?" A voice cracked on the other end.

Relief swelled through me. My words tumbled over each other, all trying to come out at once. I told him everything that happened and I pleaded with him.

"Sir, please help me," I begged.

"Put the man on the phone," he instructed. I didn't hesitate for a moment and outstretched my hand. Skeptically, the man grabbed the phone and held it to his ear. Within moments his eyes widened.

"Yes, sir," he said respectfully. "Of course, sir. Yes, sir."

Instantly, his entire demeanor changed. All the belligerence was gone. No more insults or mistreatment.

"Mr. Sulaiman, I understand your situation and apologize for this inconvenience. You are now free to go," he said

I could hardly believe it.

I gathered my things quickly, like a prisoner running

toward an open door. I just wanted to be out of that room, to not feel like I was on trial for every part of my life and every decision I had ever made. I wanted a bed. I wanted to shut my eyes and drown out the world. I wanted peace. But I still had a long way to go before I could rest easily. I collected my bags and booked the next flight from Jordan to the United States.

Now for the final hurdle. I still had one month technically left on my visa that I had used to get in the country for the training courses I attended. I told myself that if I could just pass border control, I would figure out the rest. But in the world of border control and visas, a month is cutting it close.

Nerves gathered in my belly and twisted uncomfortably as I waited in line for the next available border control agent. To the left, an agent motioned me to step forward. I forced a smile and presented my documents.

The border control agent looked over everything carefully.

"Sir, are you aware that your visa is up in just one month?" she asked.

"Yes, I know," I said.

The border control agent didn't look convinced. But I had planned for this.

"I also have this identification card if it helps," I said.

I handed over the ID badge I had been issued by the Department of Defense for the training program I had attended a few months prior. It had expired and had no relevance to my current situation, but I hoped that somehow it would speak to my character and connection to the United States.

She looked over it carefully but didn't seem to notice the expired date.

"You're free to go, sir," she said with a smile.

I nodded a thanks, grabbed my bag, and began to walk.

Maybe I should have jumped for joy and felt crazed with excitement, but more than anything, I felt tired. After months of fearing for my life every day and living with a haunting sense of dread, I was worn out. I had lived with unrelenting stress, with a roller coaster of adrenaline that had shot my nerves to pieces. Now I was safe. And safe felt a lot like wanting to sleep.

I drove directly to see my family and held them tight. I thought of the mother and son who were killed in the car accident that I should have been in. I thought of the bullet holes in the walls of my home that should have torn through my body and ended everything. I shouldn't be standing in Michigan, safe and whole, hugging my children. But I cherished every moment.

And while I savored the safety and the fact I was finally near my children, there was another reality I could not run away from.

I was starting over completely. The career I had devoted my life to building was completely gone. All the respect and prestige, all the high-level contacts, all the experience and knowledge I had sacrificed years of my life to build were now totally and utterly useless. I would need to start from scratch. I would need to build everything again from the ground up.

I had a suitcase, and I had safety. Everything else I would have to work for and earn.

But first, I needed to sleep.

CHAPTER TWELVE_

My first month in the United States felt somewhat like a very strange, long vacation. The fact I had *actually moved* had yet to sink in. It was hard for me to believe I lived *in a new country*. It had all happened so fast that I could hardly wrap my mind around the full implications of it. For the first few weeks I rested, reconnected with my family, and began the daunting task of considering the future. At forty-six years old, I was completely starting over. I looked for job opportunities and leads for work.

My brother-in-law ran a hotel remodeling and construction company, and when he learned that I had a decent skill level in handyman work, my brother-in-law invited me to come on board and work. I quickly accepted, and I worked hard and took pride in my job. I was thankful for the opportunity to earn money and begin building a new life for myself. But it was also hard. The life I built in Iraq had completely crumbled. I had nothing. No one knew that the sturdy back carrying lumber in the remodeling crew was once a pilot for dictators and dignitaries. No one knew that the stammering man struggling to say basic English words could teach an in-depth class on aerodynamics and flight safety.

As an immigrant there is a deep loss, a grief that comes with having to let go of the person you were in your home country. I was the son of a legendary man in Iraq, a highly respected and experienced pilot and flight instructor. The breadth and depth of my knowledge and experience had been hard earned over years of my life. Since the time I was barely a teenager, I had been working toward becoming a pilot. It was in my blood; it was my identity. I was flying planes before I could even drive. Almost every waking moment of my life was dedicated to being a pilot.

But all of it was suddenly irrelevant. Meaningless. Worthless. Now I was just a foreigner who needed a job and couldn't speak the language. It was humbling. And it was hard. The loss was immense. The loss of communication skills, the loss of respect and prestige, the loss of my entire household. I spent my twenties and thirties building a life for myself, making sacrifices that would hopefully pay off later down the road. I collected things, I created a life, I became somebody. I did it well. And then suddenly, it was all erased. The entire process started over.

I had to learn the language like a child, I had to find a new line of work, I had to create a new career path. But even amid loss and friction between the man I was and the man I used to be, I felt deep gratitude. I awoke every day thankful to be alive, to have the chance to see my children grow up, to not have to live in fear of death. Even the chance to start again was a gift, and I never took it for granted. I had looked at death right in the eyeballs, and I was never the same again. I realized every sunrise, every breath, every good night's sleep, every opportunity to make a living is a gift.

Slowly, but surely, I began to learn English. Necessity is a powerful motivator. I stammered through basic words and struggled to understand and master the American accent. But I got by.

One of the hotel owners we worked with decided to launch a new business venture flipping houses. He needed someone to do some of the remodeling work and asked me to come on board.

I gladly accepted. My skill set expanded quickly through experience, and I took pride in the quality of my work. Within a few months, I was earning well. But still I found myself drawn to the sky. Every time I spotted a plane in the air or heard the low hum of an aircraft, something in me ached. Every inch of me craved the rush of takeoff and the satisfaction of a smooth landing. I wanted to feel that quiet freedom of cruising through the night's sky with the world beneath me. An entire lifetime of experiences, stories, and memories sat on the shelf within my mind. I was a different person, a new man in a new country.

For the first few months of being in the United States, I didn't have a driver's license. There was a friend of my family who lived near my wife's home, and he graciously picked me up each day, dropped me off at the jobsite where I was working before going to his job. At the end of each day, my friend would come back and pick me up and bring me home. It was hard for me to rely on friends and family to get me where I needed to go, to have no independence of my own.

The thing I dreaded the most was when a customer or manager would show up to a job site to give instructions about paint color or construction details and I couldn't understand it. It was a humbling thing to stand there with a blank look on my face, to have to resort to hand motions and gestures to communicate rather than words. But somehow, I managed. I knew that if I froze to protect my pride and didn't find a way to creatively communicate, I would be out of a job. I couldn't afford to let that happen. This was survival, and I hadn't come this far to let a language barrier stop me.

Some days I felt like I would never learn the language, felt like beating my head against a thick wall that wouldn't budge. Amid these frustrations, I held onto a sense of deep gratitude for the chance to watch my children grow up, to live a full life. It made everything worth it.

My job description ranged from painter to home remodeler to lawn care worker. Any work that paid well was good work in my opinion. As soon as I saved up enough money, I hired an immigration lawyer to help me with the process of filing for political asylum. In the short term, I would need a working permission while the much longer process of obtaining political asylum was in process.

The world of paperwork and bureaucracy that was involved in obtaining everything from political asylum to a working permission, residency, or citizenship was daunting. I was grateful for the opportunity to live in the United States and wanted to make sure that I was doing things the right way. But it was an overwhelming process, and I was grateful for the guidance of my lawyer.

I received another job opportunity on a remodeling crew for an old hotel about an hour away. The project was huge. Carpets had to be ripped up, walls had to be broken down, and everything needed to be gutted. I was paid $100 a day for a full ten hours of work. I would leave my home at 7:00 a.m. each day and arrive at work at 8:00 a.m. sharp. I'd work until 6:00 p.m. and then make the hour drive back home. My only day off was Sunday. The days were long and tiring. I had no time for anything but working, sleeping, and eating.

I worked this way for an entire year—ten hours a day, six days a week. I was grateful to make the money, but it was hard and humbling work. To go from being a highly respected pilot and flight instructor to ripping up moldy carpets and replacing toilets full of sewage was a tough pill to swallow. I knew my potential, my credentials, the depth of my knowledge. But none of that mattered anymore.

Though I hate to admit it, there were a handful of times over the course of that first year that I put my head in my hands and wept. Losing my identity was deeply and indescribably painful.

Something ached in me as I pulled up that wet, moldy carpet to haul to the dumpster day after day.

Is this what it's come to? Is this who you are now?

The questions played in a loop in my head.

But each time the voices questioned, I answered.

It's better than dying. It's better than dying.

This was not a choice or a matter of preference. This was survival. I had to make it. I had to figure out a way to live and build a new life. My children needed money for school and books. I wanted them to go to college and get a good education. I wanted them to have a strong future in this new country, and as long as it depended on me, I would give them every opportunity to thrive. My children were my greatest motivation.

After working for a year on that construction project, another job opened that was closer to my house, and I gladly took it. For another six months, I worked there. Ten hours a day, six days a week. After a year and a half, I felt weary. My body was exhausted from the intense physical labor, day after day. My mind felt the fatigue of atrophy from not utilizing the knowledge I had worked so hard to acquire. I craved doing something that would wake my brain up and make me feel alive. After the life I had lived, the monotony and mindlessness of my job was tiring. Gratitude for life and thoughts of my children's future were the only fuel that kept me going.

While I was happy to be close to my children again, the reintegration process was a challenge for my wife and me. We cared for each other but had grown accustomed to living apart. She had endured so many challenges alone while I was still in Iraq. She moved to a foreign country with four children and essentially raised them as a single mom. I showed up suddenly, and it was harder than either of us imagined to pick up where we left off.

Over time it became clear there were fences we could not

mend and bridges we could not build. Living together was not a positive thing for anyone. I found a hotel room that offered monthly rental and moved in. I spent all my days working and then returned to that tiny hotel room each night. I bought a small oven so that I could cook my own meals rather than wasting money going out to eat. I needed every extra dollar for my children's future. I was happy I could give them a better, safer life, but I missed my home in Iraq. I missed having a job that made me feel alive. I missed the rush of being in the sky, the mental stimulation of improvisation. I missed the friends and family I left behind. I missed being able to speak eloquently and be easily understood.

Every time I felt the frustrations of trying to learn the language, I thought of my children who had walked the exact same path. When they arrived in the United States, they didn't speak any English. What's more, they were immediately placed in an English-speaking school and were expected to learn.

These were the days before sleek translation apps and language programs. My daughters had one dictionary and had to look up every single word for their homework assignments. Night after night, they completed the assignments through tears of fatigue and frustration. But they never gave up. It was especially difficult for my oldest daughter, Rania, as she was trying to complete her final year of high school. Her assignments were already difficult, and to be forced to translate every word by hand using a dictionary was an almost impossible task. Many tears were shed. But there was no other way. She pushed and she pushed day after day. She never threw in the towel or gave up. She graduated high school and immediately enrolled in Oakland Community College.

My second oldest daughter, Rand, also pushed herself hard to excel in academics. She studied the language and quickly learned. Within the first year, she was a straight A student in every subject, especially mathematics. The teachers placed her in a special location to take her tests just to ensure the other students didn't try to look over her shoulder and steal her answers. Once, a fellow student even pulled her aside and offered her fifty dollars to miss a few answers on her test and get a lower score because her grades were causing the rest of the class to look bad. Rand refused to do so. She had worked incredibly hard for her achievements, and she wasn't about to compromise her integrity for a little money. She graduated in the top ten of her class, and she was accepted to numerous schools around the United States for an accredited PharmD program to become a pharmacist. She decided on the one in Michigan and began school at age nineteen.

After enrolling in Wayne State University, she moved into my little hotel room with me, and we lived together while she completed her PharmD program. For six months we stayed together in that little room. After a few months, my son Rami also joined us. Three people, two beds, and very limited floor space. We were more cramped than cozy, but we didn't complain. I was alive and I had work. My daughter had the opportunity to go to a great college with a bright career ahead of her. We made the best of it.

But it only took forty-eight hours for me to start shopping for an apartment, which provided a proper kitchen and bedroom for each of us. After living in such a tight space, the new apartment felt like a palace. We each had our own bed and enough kitchen space to prepare proper meals. I saved enough money to buy my daughter a car to make her commute back and forth to school easier. I wanted to give her whatever tools necessary to succeed. Every day we would rise together, and she would drive me to the hotel jobsite where I would work all day while she went to school. When she finished, she would drive back and pick me up, and then we'd go back to our apartment to eat and sleep before waking up to do it all over again.

We found a sort of camaraderie during that time in each other. Father and daughter sharing a starter apartment and a vehicle. Both of us working hard, both of us struggling to make something of ourselves in a new country. It was an equalizer of sorts—putting us on the same level and creating a strong bond between us.

In 2008, I was hired for a full-time position as a hotel maintenance worker. I gave it my all. Anything that needed to be done, I did—from pool maintenance to replacing lost key cards to filling in for the breakfast staff or running to the grocery store to get food items for the hotel. I became quick friends with the staff and guests. I laughed and talked and never complained.

There were days when I had thoughts of who I used to be and the career I used to have, and it would hit me like a punch in the gut. But I always reminded myself of the bullet holes in the wall that should have been in my flesh. I brushed it off, kept my head down, and pressed on, grateful for life.

At the end of that year, a new opportunity came along. A friend recommended me for a position to serve as a cultural advisor for the United States military. As a pilot and former officer in the Iraqi Army, I had a unique perspective that would be of great value to troops in training before deployment to the Middle East. For three years, my only value was being an able body that could move heavy things, paint walls, and make repairs. All the rich knowledge in my mind laid dormant, and I longed to see it resurrected.

I had also been given a front row seat to witness good American men and women give their all to bring freedom and liberation to oppressed people. Had it not been for the United States, Saddam's brutal regime might have continued and caused even greater harm to innocent people. I was forced to flee my own country and leave everything overnight because of violence and unrest. I could only hope that my country would see better days, that the next generation wouldn't have to face these same struggles. I wanted to help in any way I could. I applied for the job and was immediately accepted. Some embers in my mind and soul that I thought had gone cold suddenly ignited. I had a mission and a purpose again, and that felt good.

My assignment was to help educate and prepare troops for what they would be facing during deployment. I pulled back the curtain and gave them an inside look into the culture, mindset, and strategies they would be up against.

I maintained my position with the hotel as I was only needed every month or two for the consulting position. I would go on assignment to help with a ten-day training and then return and work at the hotel until the military needed me again. I explained the situation to my superiors at the hotel, and they understood. Since it was for the military, it was a good cause in their eyes. For the better part of a year, I managed to juggle both my position at the hotel and as a consultant. There were weeks when I was exhausted. I would go from teaching and conducting intense training right into working to get caught up at the hotel. My mind was pulled in all directions constantly.

In 2009, consulting requests started coming more and more often and lasting even longer. It became harder and harder for me to juggle both positions. I felt like I was always tired, always running from behind at the hotel. It was time for another transition, and I began to search for a replacement for my position at the hotel. I found the perfect person to take my position, trained them thoroughly, and phased out of the job. I was finally free to consult as often as I was asked.

I loved my job. I took great honor and pride in being able to meaningfully contribute to the American military and play a small role in bringing freedom and peace to the side of the world I now called home.

But in 2011 came another twist. President Obama gave the order to withdraw troops from Iraq. There were no longer mass amounts of troops preparing for deployment and thus no need for a cultural consultant. I was suddenly without a job. But with my contacts in the hotel industry, it didn't take long for me to find work. I worked a remodeling job for a few months and then landed a steady position with Comfort Suites in 2012, a job I held until 2019.

Life seemed to finally be stable for me. I had a consistent job and routine. I bought a house and renovated it beautifully. I had friends and family. I had made a life for myself that I had learned to love. But in 2020 came another unexpected twist. I was involved in a car accident that injured my shoulder and back. The pain was almost unbearable. I was forced to get surgery and couldn't work for months. I stayed at home, trying to heal as fast as I could. But there was no way to speed up the healing process. It simply would take as long as it takes. After all those years of working nonstop, I would have thought I would relish the downtime. But I missed having a purpose. It was hard for me to sit alone at home, day after day, with nothing to do.

Slowly, but surely, I regained my strength and began to recover, but my shoulder still hurt constantly. The doctors pushed me to have an operation to fix it, but I resisted. If I had the operation, it could interfere with my ability to fly. After moving to the United States, I hadn't been able to fly, but the thought of never being able to do it again hurt more than the chronic pain of my shoulder. I am a pilot, first and foremost. So I held out and endured the discomfort.

I arrived in the United States with only a suitcase and built my life and career, brick by brick, until it was sturdy and reliable. But I felt a far more intense pride in watching my children thrive than in my own accomplishments. They were given the difficult task of arriving in a foreign country during their formative and educational years and having to forge their own paths. Against all odds, each of them rose to incredible success both in their personal and professional lives.

My oldest daughter, Rania, decided that being a pharmacist wasn't for her and changed majors. She earned her bachelor's degree in medical life science, and she went on to become a wildly successful physician's assistant and fell in love with a handsome medical engineer.

My second daughter, Rand, completed her PhD. She graduated with honors from her class, and I fought back tears of pride as I watched her take the stage and receive her diploma. She followed the path all the way to becoming a licensed pharmacist and moved to Indiana.

My son, Rami, finished school and attended Oakland University where he earned his bachelor's degree in electrical engineering. He was then hired for a prestigious job at British Aerospace Engineering, which worked with the United States government to build and improve military tanks, and he even got the bragging rights of having a license to drive a tank.

My youngest daughter, Rula, attended Oakland University and became a licensed dietician. She enjoyed working in the health and wellness industry for a while, but she couldn't shake the feeling she was made for more. She made the bold and brave decision to go back to school and earn a law degree.

Watching each of my children pursue their own unique career path made those years of sacrifice and hard work worth it for me. The life I had dreamed for them, the opportunities I had hoped to give them, they were living.

One of the greatest things about the United States of America is the fact that it is a nation that opens its arms to foreigners and immigrants, something that has been at the foundation of American history since its beginning. But becoming a citizen of the United States and assimilating into the culture is not an easy task—not only in terms of learning the language and culture, but also working to get permanent residency.

In 2006, I began the long road toward getting my green card. Given the circumstances, I started by filing for political asylum. I did everything by the book, provided every necessary document that was requested, and appeared at every appointment. But years went by without closure. Each year, I was sure it was my year, and each time I was disappointed. More paperwork, more wait time for processing, more interviews.

I thought my situation seemed like a clear case for political asylum. I had fled my country under the threat of death to join my family in the United States. But despite how straightforward the situation appeared to be, there seemed to be no end to the long process of obtaining asylum.

As the years dragged on, my daughter came to me with a new proposition. By this time, she had obtained legal residency and was over twenty-one years old, which made her eligible to be my sponsor for a green card under the heading of "Family Reunification," a process that allows legal United States residents to reunite with close immigrant family members. This process still took time, but eventually it worked. Even so, it wasn't until 2019 that I received my green card. It took nearly thirteen years to get. Even at the time of the writing of this book, I still have another two years to receive an American passport because there is a five-year waiting period after getting permanent residence.

The process of becoming a citizen is certainly not for the faint of heart. It didn't matter that I consulted for the United States military or had a son who worked with the government. It didn't matter how hard I worked or what I did to try to speed up the process. The road to becoming a US citizen is laden with thick bureaucracy.

Even still, I will always be thankful for the opportunity to live in the United States and give my children a better future. Once upon a time, America used to be referred to as "the land of opportunity," and I have seen that to be true firsthand. The opportunities are abundant. But reaching out and grabbing hold of them, especially as an immigrant, requires grit, perseverance, and bravery. It requires you to work for every inch you're given. That's what I did, and that's what my children did.

And my life and the lives of my children have changed forever.

I had no idea what the future would bring when I boarded the plane to come to the United States. I only knew I didn't want to die. I would be the first to tell you that starting over in a foreign country is not an easy task. It was humbling and it was hard, but I would also tell you that it was worth it. It was worth every early morning and late night. Worth every strained conversation I struggled to have in English. Worth living in a hotel room for. The pride I had to swallow was nothing in comparison to the immense pride I feel in being a citizen of the United States and seeing my children thrive.

For that, I am forever grateful.

CHAPTER THIRTEEN_

Perhaps there are those who would call my life uncommon or extraordinary. And there are fragments of truth to be found in that assessment. Not many people have flown into a sandstorm or landed in Somalia in the middle of a military coup. Not many people have seen a brutal dictator in his underwear or had their house shot to pieces in an assassination attempt.

For me, these are simply my experiences. The things that shaped me, the things that made me who I am today. And while many of these specific experiences are not widely shared by others, there are many aspects of my story that were born out of the same desires, struggles, and challenges that every single human faces.

Throughout history, humans have had to navigate the difficult path of what it means to live under an oppressive government like I did. To grapple with what it means to maintain personal integrity under leadership that is evil and corrupt. To try to create a life worth being proud of for you and your children in the midst of circumstances that are anything but ideal.

Anyone who is a parent knows what it means to make tough sacrifices to create a better future for their children, just like I do. We know the instinctual fire in the belly that empowers us to move mountains and cross oceans for our children, the kind of love that keeps us up at night, that makes us forget our pain in the pursuit of giving our children a better life than the one we were handed.

Anyone who has had to create a new life as an immigrant in a foreign country knows the challenges of learning a new language and culture. We know the grief that comes with leaving an entire life behind, of saying goodbye to the identity of who you once were in your homeland. We know the humility it takes to struggle through broken sentences, to take on hard jobs to provide for our families. We know the longing to communicate and connect, to be respected and understood. We know the bravery and fortitude it takes to start from nothing and build a future one layer at a time.

And anyone who has had the value of being given a second chance to live and an opportunity to start again knows the deep gratitude that comes with every sunrise, every new day. Each morning when I open my eyes, I think of the thousand times I should have died and didn't. I cherish the air that fills my lungs and the opportunity to see my children grow and succeed.

Every time I hold my grandchildren near, I think of the

world they are being born into and the future that awaits them. I think of the ways my wife and I struck out and pioneered the way, like explorers creating a path through thick jungle. I think of how our children followed in our footsteps, overcoming obstacles, paving the way for their children who would follow.

It's easy to want to put people in boxes, to label experiences and make judgements based on them. But in my experience, life is not like that. Life isn't nice and neat or easy to navigate. Impressions of a person aren't always correct.

Depending on what time in my life I would've met you, you would have gotten vastly different impressions of me.

You could have met me smiling next to Saddam Hussein or preparing a group of US military recruits for deployment. You could have met me at a dinner with famous world leaders or in a motel room trying to cook dinner for myself on a portable stove.

You could have met me on a construction site struggling to put a sentence together in English or in front of a class teaching aerodynamics. You could have met me expertly piloting a massive aircraft or in a border control line begging for refuge in a foreign country.

Depending on the chapter of my life that you could have entered, you would have formed a different sketch of Mohammed Sulaiman. You would have formed different impressions, come to different conclusions.

But they are all me.

All the seasons of life that I journeyed through are all pieces of me that fit together to create who I am today.

We as humans cannot categorize each other or place each

other within the straitjacket of their first impressions and quick assumptions. We need to keep an open mind, take a second look, be open to different perspectives and points of view.

As I look back, I don't have regrets. Mistakes to be sure, but no regrets. I've lived a full life and have done the best that I could with what I was given at each step of the way.

But I do have a wish.

I want to return to the sky before I die. I want to feel the rush of taking off a runway, feel the freedom of flight, feel the power of piloting an aircraft.

Some people talk about being destined to do something in life; they talk of having a purpose or calling. And while I cannot speak to the will of God for my life, I can tell you this:

I was born to fly.

Just as surely as I know my name is Mohammed Sulaiman. That I was born in Iraq and now call Michigan my home. That I love my children and cherish my grandchildren.

I know that I was born to fly.

It is in my blood and in my veins. Woven into the fabric of my being.

I am, I always was, and I always will be a pilot.

ACKNOWLEDGMENTS_

Lauren:

First of all, I'd like to thank Hamody Jasim a.k.a The Terrorist Whisperer and Jeff Morris. Without you boys meeting on Haifa Street in the most unlikely of ways, this whole thing might never have happened.

My editor, Kyle; my talented cover designer, Jenneth; and my formatting guru, Ben, for all your hard work to produce this final product. You guys are the best.

Mohammed, for such a great ride these past few years while working together—your sense of humor, positive attitude, and perspective on life made the process so enjoyable. My kids for being my biggest fans in the world.

And last but not least, my amazing husband, Eralp—for your love and unwavering support, for bringing me endless cups of coffee to fuel the writing process, and for willingly participating in countless hours of crazy read-aloud editing sessions. The journey is better with you!

Mohammed:

Thank you NMSTARS—without you I might never have had the courage to tell my story. Hamody Jasim for supporting me and connecting me with the perfect writer. And to Lauren—thank you for writing my story. It's been a true pleasure working with you.

ALSO BY LAUREN UNGELDI_

LEGION RISING

Not everyone has pulled shards of another man's skull from the palm of their hand. Not everyone has stood over the bodies of friends whose lives were lost in an instant. Not everyone has struggled to face their own reflection for years on end.

But anyone who has experienced trauma or adversity will resonate with *Legion Rising*, the unflinchingly honest account of an army officer's journey through combat in the Iraq War and rising beyond the scars that trauma leaves behind.

Experience an honest, unedited, and occasionally humorous glimpse of the rigors of military training through Jeff's eyes. Follow Jeff through up-close, fast-paced accounts of the thrills and dangers of combat as a Platoon Leader in Iraq. Feel the weight of the gruesome and tragic loss of eight men whose lives were lost in the line of duty. Journey with Jeff through his battle to face the scars and shadows that followed him long after his time serving in the military was over.

Through Jeff's authentic voice and brave transparency, readers will be drawn into his story and find themselves able to relate to his struggle and ultimate rise from adversity.

This is not simply a military memoir, it's a memoir of life—of tragedy, healing, and leadership. Through the heart-pounding stories of combat to the transparent and personal look into the process of healing, a message emerges—one that will inspire people across all walks of life.

Not Those People

Not Those People is the true story of one man's journey battling drug addiction and mental health challenges in a small Pennsylvania town.

In this unexpectedly transparent account of falling into addiction as a teenager and the spiral toward a total loss of control that followed, Zak Maiden shines light on the hidden battles that are being fought by everyday Americans across the nation.

The book offers a raw and intimate view into the complexities of addiction and the road to recovery by dismantling the stigmas that surround those who deal with these things. Through the eyes of an everyday, small town boy comes a story shining a spotlight on the war that countless people wage every day in silence, because they are afraid to be honest about their struggles with the labels that society has attached to them.

No one wants to be those people. The depressed people. The addicted people. The suicidal people. The people who are society's failures and misfits.

Through Zak's acutely relatable story, comes a path toward a new wave of transparency and opens up conversations around topics of addiction and mental health.

This book is equal parts story, diary, and invitation to bring the hidden struggles of people all over America out of the shadows and into the light. To abolish stigmas and normalize conversations around topics of mental health and drug recovery. To prove that we are all just human. That we all face challenges.

That we are not outcasts and misfits.

We are Not Those People.

LEGACY OF AN ENTREPRENEUR

What Legacy are You Leaving Behind?

Entrepreneur: A person who organizes or operates a business, taking on financial risk with the hopes of earning a profit.

What you hold in your hands is a guidebook. A map of sorts.

Is there a spark in you waiting to be ignited? An idea? A business venture you can't get out of your mind? A safety net you are ready to leave behind? This book is for you.

If you operate a business and are challenged by the difficulty of passing it to the next generation, this book is for you.

The world of entrepreneurship is an exciting one, filled with opportunity. But it can be scary, confusing, and even lonely. Learn from someone who has faced it all before.

Entrepreneur Robert E. Ness tells his story of starting ODW Logistics with a dream and little pocket money, growing it, and passing it on to the next generation. His transparency, humor, practicality, and wisdom gained through both successes and struggles will inspire you to step forward and put your dreams into action.

How do you deal with setbacks and heartbreaks?

How do you respond when the risk nearly does you in?

How do you navigate complications and sensitivities when family dynamics intertwine with business?

Family business can be a great gift. And it can get really messy, especially when the family business and the business of the family collide. Bob's principles, lessons, and hard-learned wisdom offer hope, practical take-aways, and guidance to you as you embark on your journey.

This book will help you make moves, take risks, and make your dreams a reality and ultimately leave behind a legacy to bless those who come after you.

ABOUT THE AUTHORS_

Lauren Ungeldi is a celebrated bestselling author, CEO, and devout believer in the power of storytelling. She is passionate about highlighting heroes, overcomers, and remarkable leaders all over the world by bringing their stories to life on the page.

If she's not writing, she's probably exploring a foreign country, on a hike, jumping out of an airplane, or eating something delicious.

Mohammed Sulaiman is the former pilot to Saddam Hussein and member of the Iraqi air force.

He now works as a consultant for the United States military and resides near his children and grandchildren.

www.ingramcontent.com/pod-product-compliance
Lightning Source LLC
Chambersburg PA
CBHW030656060526
44119CB00097B/463/J